Russell Lucas is a UK-based artist specialising in writing, devising, producing, acting and directing original work. His medium is predominantly theatre, but he also creates online content that studies the journey of other theatremakers.

Recent work includes the series *Theatremakers* with Digital Theatre+, *The Bobby Kennedy Experience*, *Warped* at VAULT Festival, the American Season at Canal Café, *An Evening Without Kate Bush* at Soho Theatre and on tour, and *Julie Madly Deeply* Off-Broadway, in Edinburgh and the West End.

Russell is a qualified lecturer and has written and delivered workshops for the Donmar Warehouse, East 15 Acting School, Rose Bruford College of Theatre and Performance, the National Youth Theatre, the Verbier Festival in Switzerland, and Hyundai in South Korea.

Russell Lucas

300
THOUGHTS FOR
THEATREMAKERS

A Manifesto for the
Twenty-First-Century Theatremaker

Foreword by Alan Lane

NICK HERN BOOKS
London
www.nickhernbooks.co.uk

A Nick Hern Book

300 Thoughts for Theatremakers
first published in Great Britain in 2022
by Nick Hern Books Limited,
The Glasshouse, 49a Goldhawk Road,
London W12 8QP

Cover image © Shutterstock/Mrspopman1985
Designed and typeset by Nick Hern Books
Printed and bound in Great Britain by
TJ Books Limited

A CIP catalogue record for this book is available
from the British Library

ISBN 978 1 84842 997 0

MIX
Paper from
responsible sources
FSC® C013056
www.fsc.org

Contents

For Ana
(*She'll know why*)

'The actor, his muscles humming like a live wire,
his voice thundering with a revivified resonance,
his instincts sharp as the cutting edge of a laser beam,
his sensibility imploding with original perceptions and
a readiness to communicate a fresh vision of the postnuclear world,
will take the stage again, and a new theatrical age will dawn.'

Charles Marowitz

Foreword

Alan Lane

> *'Thought #131: Did you ever get taught how to set up a theatre company? Me neither.'*

'Theatre' is a small word for an amazingly rich and varied practice. Andrew Lloyd Webber makes theatre. Selina Thompson makes theatre. Forced Entertainment makes theatre. Russell Lucas makes theatre. I make theatre.

Russell Lucas and I live in very different theatre worlds. I have loved reading about Russell's world in this book. His passion, his practical wisdom, his indestructible optimism. How could someone with all that at his disposal fail to make theatre that people want to watch?

> *'Thought #195: There are many, many artists out there who do not have funding, yet still find a way – but this thought won't chime with the funded, as they seem to presume that you can only work in the arts if you have funding.'*

The theatre world is under real pressure. What with the cuts to arts in state schools, the increasing cost of attending drama school, and the overall crisis in arts funding, there is less space than ever for independent, audience-focused theatremakers like Russell.

But what this book demonstrates so clearly is that whatever happens, however catastrophic the effects of this current culture war, there will always be theatremakers. Battered by the forces that question their worth, that attempt to make them subservient to institutions, or (as Russell explains in Thought #249) reduce them to tick-boxes, they remain unrepentant, never tamed.

When everything else is in crisis and penury, a theatremaker will find a light and a costume – and get on with the job of entertaining, of provoking, of inspiring. Thank God. Thank God for all the theatremakers like Russell who, with clear-eyed conviction, set about the age-old job of sharing a space with people and telling them a story. And thank God for this book, because it will surely be a comfort and support to all those who follow in Russell's independent and determined footsteps.

To the theatremakers!

Alan Lane is Artistic Director of Slung Low, an award-winning theatre company based in Leeds, specialising in making large-scale productions in non-theatre spaces with community performers at their heart. During the Covid pandemic, the company was the ward lead for social-care referrals and ran a non-means-tested food bank. The experiences are recorded in Alan's book The Club on the Edge of Town: A Pandemic Memoir, *published in 2022.*

Introduction

Who Am I?

I'd like to begin by explaining why I've written a book about making theatre, because technically it shouldn't exist – at least not by me. I'm not famous, nor am I prolific. I'm a relatively unknown theatremaker with one GCSE and no degree. See, with my background you're really not supposed to work in the arts – never mind be successful and then write a book about it.

Of course, I'm being glib, as we're *all* allowed to work in the theatre, but that message doesn't always get through to society – let alone to the lost artists who've been encouraged to 'Go get a real job.'

Take my journey, for example: I come from Clacton-on-Sea in Essex, where it's all about economic survival – and back in the seventies and eighties it *really* was. When you reached your sixteenth birthday you were expected to work in a chip shop or on the pier and that was you done. You'd peaked. Any deeper discussions about utilising your existing skill set or having a career… Well, there were no debates on either of those, as no one knew what they were and we probably couldn't afford them anyway. Dreams were for the rich. So, one week after my sixteenth birthday, I began real-jobbing in my local chippy, The Plaice To Be, and one week and one hour after my sixteenth birthday, I silently whispered: 'This isn't the place for me.'

Admittedly, I didn't know where I wanted to go next or how to get there but, as it turns out, it's enough to keep pulling at a thread, because I'm here now, working in the arts, despite society telling me that I couldn't, and my parents saying that I probably shouldn't.

From a very early age, every time I went into a theatre I felt completely at home. Its magic, its possibilities and its warmth were palpable to me. I wanted to live and work in there for ever, and thanks to my teenage whisper finally finding a voice, I got there. Here.

So, how did I do it? And how can you make a successful and long career in the arts? Well, what type of career do you want?

One piece of immediate advice I can offer you is that you should resolve right now that, no matter what, you're going to stick around. You should also acknowledge you really do wish to live your life in the theatre. It's only then – after you've given voice to your ambition – that the flimsy, self-imposed barriers that have stopped you from seeing the theatre as a real job will melt away.

Next, you need to redefine two words: 'industry' and 'success'. These two nouns are responsible for so many artists falling by the wayside because they seemingly couldn't get into the industry nor achieve success. So let's redefine them.

'Success', from this point forward, will be when you have begun to take steps towards achieving an income from your artistic work; and the 'industry' will now be called your 'trade'.

Now, I acknowledge that your path won't be an easy one – but that's one reason why we all feel so at home in the theatre, isn't it? We're not regular people, nor do we seek the 'normal' life. We desire creativity, freedom, stories, illusion, applause, a team, agency, travel – in fact: a life filled with imagination. Every day.

So, suit up; for you *are* allowed to work in the theatre.

Who Are the Theatremakers?

A theatremaker is anyone involved in the making of theatre. Whether you are a director, actor, writer, designer or another creative, this – of course – makes you a maker of theatre. This book speaks directly to all of these roles as individuals and to its collective noun. The person who uses the term 'theatremaker' is a hybrid artist, a creative soul that can turn their hand to anything to get their show on.

I consider myself to be a theatremaker as I make theatre using my own resources. I come up with an idea, rehearse it, find a suitable platform, and then sell tickets however I can. I have no regular team, I've never used a set, sound or costume designer (yet), and I generally operate the lights myself. I write, produce, improvise, teach and choreograph. I'm also quite deft at finding cheap props online and can make trailers, posters and GIFs for publicity. Plus I know how to remove red wine from a costume (use white). I'm not rich and don't come from money (can you tell?), and I don't possess the urge to climb a career ladder either, nor become a prolific artist; and curiously I've never applied for public funding. I just make theatre. In a room. Any room. I theatricalise my idea and put it in front of an audience. For the most part, my ideas manifest on a live platform, sometimes online or like now, as a book.

I've staged work in New York, Toronto, London and Tipton, and in 2018 I made an online interview series with Digital Theatre+ that's streamed into schools around the world. I've directed art gallery films, commissioned an American playwright with an independent venue in London, and devised a new play with the same team over three years. Oh, and everyone's always been paid.

Sounds professional, doesn't it? Well, it is. So who am I? Well, I'm definitely not 'Fringe', as that's a reductive term used by the misinformed to describe and supposedly locate artists who, at some point, must surely be aiming for the 'Centre' (be honest). Nor am I commercial. No. I am an independent theatremaker, and you won't have heard of me because I don't exist – at least not under the regular terminology of 'director', 'producer', 'actor' or 'writer', terms that don't really represent my skill set any more, and so I rarely use them.

Theatremakers are like the 'Where's Wally?' of the arts – we're here, but you have to look really hard to find us. We'll pop up at festivals (a lot), but you'll rarely see us on the popular stages, as our transient nature could be performing cabaret or dance one week, then borrowing from the conventions of mime or puppetry the next; and that's hard to categorise using the regular ways of classification. Maybe we're indefinable?

So how did we manifest? By the continued slashing of budgets, changes of policies within funded theatres, and the ever-persistent commercial sector sucking up the air through the vacuum of nostalgia and film? It's a theory.

How about our extended periods of unemployment as we wait for 'heavy-pencilled' jobs to turn into half a day's work? (#actorslife) What about that devious myth that there are too many artists and not enough places for them to perform? Couple that with the cold hard truth of not enough affordable rehearsal spaces, outlandish financial demands on our already delicate reality – and how long was it going to be before we grabbed hold of the reins? Again.

In the same way that the actor-managers of the nineteenth century morphed into the director, the theatremaker is the next aggregation of the desires of the actor. And this seismic evolution/revolution was born from our exclusion from too many parties – for all those times we should have been the hosts, we were miscast as the caterers. And now that the theatremaker roams freely, they have discovered that the theatre itself needed them, before it too became a muted servant.

Theatremakers no longer spend days waiting for permission to cross the Rubicon to that utopian centre. No. We have walked off down the road and created our own trade, and us Jills and us Jacks of all the trades are fast becoming the majority.

Maybe one day, the birth of theatremakers – and their dirty ways – will be studied in schools, paving the way for more like us? Imagine the possibilities.

So, let it be known: the theatre is being reoccupied by its original tenant: The Maker of Theatre. And if you're salivating right now, come join us off the radar. You can plough up the stalls, erase the interval and even tie some knots in the curtains if you wish, because it's your trade too. But be warned: you'll need to tear the tickets, serve the drinks, bring up the lights, and then go break everyone's heart with your self-penned aria. Yes, it's back to the old ways: make a show, sell your tickets, make some money, then make a new show.

Spread the word: the theatremaker is now the centre.

How to Use This Book

The endless academic theories on the making of performance don't chime with me much, so *300 Thoughts for Theatremakers* is more of a practical, grassroots, help-yourself book on the endless minutiae of live art-making that I have observed or used over the years. It is not a method, nor a practice, and I am not your teacher. It's more of an accessible sense-making tool whereby you can drop in occasionally for a provocation or a reflective moment which may usher you along to your next decision.

Some of the thoughts give specific examples of my experience, others offer up ways towards clarity. Most, however, are designed to shunt you – the career-driven, professional artist – towards an independent way of thinking, whilst I secretly slip out the back door leaving you to your own discoveries.

The book has five parts in total, each containing sixty thoughts. Some of my musings slot nicely into specific sections, but, because the making of theatre is a holistic process, some sit comfortably in any one of the sections.

The three hundred thoughts are jumping-off points, they are provocations, and whilst you may not agree with all of them, I merely seek to encourage new thinking, debate, discussion – and maybe some disagreement. It's full of contradictions and if it wasn't, I'd be very worried, as there is no one way to make theatre, but there are a million new questions to ask.

The future of theatre will belong to the maverick minds who possess the skills to mix things up and who have enough tools in their box to trick the game. In fact, I'd say that you and I – the Trojan horses of theatre – are required now more than ever.

PART 1

MAKING
THEATRE

The mandatory elements required to make theatre can be tricky to pin down because first we need to establish what actually qualifies as a piece of theatre.

My friend, the performer Ana Mirtha Sariego, says that theatre is an illusion. I wholeheartedly agree. I'd add that it must also be a live act with at least one performer present – and my inner-hippie would like to conclude that it's a form of mass-meditation, whereby the audience all sit in silence receiving a specific discussion on life.

But now the shape-shifting theatremaker has arrived, bending the rules and operating inside a system they've built for themselves. Will they also use new techniques to make work, thus redefining the theatrical act?

Well, be careful, my friends. Therein lies 'The Artist's Trap'. Just because we can make theatre our own way, we must not forget that we are still an amalgamation of all of the traditional skill sets, and – like the multi-million-pound musical – we too serve the audience and the sale of the ticket.

More inside…

WHAT DOES THE WORLD NEED?

Before you make some new theatre – stop. Park your idea for a moment and ask yourself: 'What does the world need from the theatre right now?'

As a theatremaker, you should – in fact you *must* – learn to foster a mindset whereby you can divine what the world currently needs. This isn't necessarily about making something that represents what is happening now – that lives in the realm of documentary which probably (truthfully) will be happier on screen or radio. No, discovering and then devising the world's next piece of groundbreaking *theatre* is embedded in you being able to tap into the zeitgeist – to the world around you, to the one that you can see and feel.

But how do you conjure this skill?

I suspect everyone must find their own way to tune in. But to hear and answer the call to arms, first you must learn to listen to the questions and cries from humanity. Does the world need political art right now? Protest? Fun? Clowning? And what about the theatre: what does it need? Another *Hamilton*? More verbatim work? Fewer autobiographical shows?

Answer some of the above, and you will begin to create theatre with a responsibility to the 'Now'.

WHAT DOES THE
WORLD NOT NEED?

Still, pausing for a second, I want to share a secret with you: there is a real desire inside some producers of theatre to repeat what has come before.

You only need to study the plethora of failed jukebox musicals that followed *Mamma Mia!* and the opulent, Wagnerian shows that snapped at the heels of *Phantom of the Opera* and *Les Misérables* to note the many challenges to their thrones. As of today, though, those top-three musicals still reign supreme in the West End. Why? Because we don't (truthfully) need any more of them. Sure, there have been a few shows that maybe lasted seven or eight years and were deemed to be 'hits', but that's usually down to financial backing rather than a never-ending audience demand and any specific artistic contribution to the genre.

Take *Mamma Mia!*, for example. It's the pioneer of the modern jukebox musical and perfectly captures a particular audience's desire. I remember thinking in 1999, when it opened, that it is a flimsy plot with some ABBA songs attached, and that it was not a musical – but it has proved to be a brilliant partnering of hit songs and it tapped into a zeitgeist. Coupled with an astute marketing campaign, and *voilà*, the genre of jukebox musical was reborn again. A theatrical *coup d'état*.

I guess it makes sense to copy it. You see a formula working really well and find a way to reuse it again. And again. But whilst this is tempting and can (on occasion) be financially lucrative, I believe replicating an existing piece of theatre will always be short-lived. It will create a career based on the past, rather than one that wishes to renew the theatre and remain relevant inside its ecosystem.

If you want to make the 'Next Big Thing', you are going to need to bend a genre, repackage it, and then bring something new to the table. We need it.

3 WHY NOW?

Now you have an idea for your show, let's hold its feet to the fire for a moment.

The most effective theatre – in fact, the most impactful art – is the one that answers the question: 'Why now?' Why does this piece exist now in its current time? So, before you even go into pre-production, ask yourself: 'Why am I even making this show now?'

Yes, you could say 'Because I want to make it' (which is actually the *reason* you're making it), but the shows that survive the decades are the ones that are relevant to mankind and to the world, which are not only snapshots of their time, but also include one or many of the never-ending problems of living. Identify and focus on these elements in your show and your piece might be studied and revived for years, and if you include the human condition and family dynamics, you're more than halfway there.

Here's an example. Your show is 'about your childhood'. Great. I'm sure it's interesting and everyone you know will love it. Your family and friends will buy tickets and cry at the opening. But they are not your true audience – not

if you wish to live a long professional life in the arts.

Your true audience is the people you *don't* know. But how do you reach them? By showing them a world they understand, have heard about, or are interested in; by creatively discussing – not teaching – your show's topic in such a unique way that they discover something new about themselves and the world; by finding the humanity inside your story, the loneliness, the joy of childhood, and the pitfalls of maturity. Do all that and you will have answered some of the audience's silent thoughts: 'Why am I watching this now?' 'Why am I giving you ninety minutes of my life and fifteen pounds?' and: 'I want to learn.'

If you don't at least attempt to answer these questions, your work could be quickly forgotten – and you don't want to be forgotten, do you? Solve all of the above, and the audience will not only cry at your show – they'll fund your next one.

WHAT'S THE DISCUSSION?

Whenever you start work on a new piece of theatre, you'll have an idea of what your show is about or based on. For instance:

'A moment in my life.'
'That time I watched someone unlawfully deported.'
'The life of Charlie Chaplin.'

Amazing. You've started. Your idea is here and after asking 'Why now?' of your project, you must move forward by identifying the *discussion* within the show.

I learned this wonderful framing device on a workshop with Lois Weaver from the theatre company Split Britches, where she asked us: 'What do you want to discuss in your show?' This then extended into 'What do you really, *really* want to discuss?' and so on. For me, this was a beautiful, contemporary way to re-ask the old-fashioned questions: 'What is my show about?' and 'What is its message?' – but on a much deeper, intelligent level. By using Lois's concept of discussion over 'It's about…' raises your focus, creating an enticing and intelligent invitation for your audience.

Let's take 'A moment in my life'. Having boiled down your discussion you might be surprised to learn that you actually want to make a show discussing how parental errors can be cyclical; or the concept of blame; or the physical things parents buy children that represent their ideas and values. If you're making a show 'about Charlie Chaplin', you might find you actually want to discuss the way women's voices were also muted *off*-camera in the silent era.

Find the contemporary, relevant discussion within your work – and it will further nourish you and answer 'Why now?'

ALLOW PROJECTS TO FERMENT

Don't worry if you're currently 'frozen' or 'stuck' on your project. It's important to allow your ideas to fester, compost and mature.

I once had a show idea I named *Ghost Bollocks*. I knew I wanted to use the image of the classic white-sheeted ghost, but that was all. That was back in 2015. It's now 2021 that I'm writing this, and although we've had a few exploratory days, nothing concrete has evolved. Yet. Now is not the time. Yes, we've had lots of fun creating some really interesting imagery and content, but (for now) we've walked away from it, resolving to let it soak for a while and wait for the moment when the world needs it. This is very important for two reasons. One – if we really had a burning desire to make it now, we'd do it. And two – we haven't solved the 'Why now?' of the project.

I actually don't mind this bump in the road, as it's all part of the process. Sometimes projects just need the world to require them, or for you to catch up – either way, it's all fine. Put it on the shelf until you're ready and don't worry if someone else creates something similar – it'll be nothing like yours.

WORKING TITLES

It's super-useful to allow yourself to riff and remain fluid with the title of your piece; to not quite find its real name straight away. But how do you get to that space?

I made an educational show once that we provisionally called 'Teen'. It was the code word we used to talk about it, but we knew it would never be the actual title. The real name arrived (*The Pregnancy Project*), once we'd found the discussion of the piece and created some solid content.

Try the age-old free-writing concept whereby you have to keep coming up with show titles for two minutes without taking your pen off the page – resulting in hundreds of names that might work for your show. Allow yourself to give it the worst and the best titles. Let it all come out whilst remaining mindful of the discussion within that you are hoping to have. Next, leave it alone for a while, and then go back to it, choose a few that you like and try and boil them down to one. This can now be your working title, but don't raise it up to the echelons of 'The Show Title' yet because it may still feel like it has to earn its place. Even when you are in the thick of rehearsals, it's okay if you still want to hold off.

Of course, if you are nearing a deadline then you may not have the luxury of time, but you can still go through the process of having your show's title earn its place; albeit it in a faster way.

SET UP
SHOP ASAP

Sometimes it's really useful to announce your idea or your project early on. I do this as a kind of warning shot – a line in the sand, as it were; staking my claim on a topic. It may not happen for a few years, but I just go for it. It usually feels amazing, plus it'll more than likely instigate a healthy inner conflict inside me, forcing me to interrogate the project further.

By committing to it so blatantly it may then start to manifest itself as an image, a social-media post, or even a scene released on a website. This will get people to talk to you about it – applying some light pressure on you to really think about if you do want to make it.

It's okay if you don't make it, by the way. But hey – if this gesture moves you onto the next stage (whatever that is), it's all good, right?

NO MESSAGES

Why is theatre so bad sometimes? You know the drill – you applaud, you go to the bar, smile graciously, and then travel home with a foggy head wondering why you just paid for your own death.

I have a theory. It's because the audience is not actually needed in the room. The theatremaker has gone so far up the tree they've forgotten about the spectators below who are waiting for some apples. But, so as not to unbalance the fragility of the climb, the audience waits dutifully, looking skyward in the hope something will finally drop. If it doesn't, they'll be on the bus one minute after your final curtain.

So, how do you avoid this? Well, you must remain connected to one of your major responsibilities: that you serve the audience. They are your boss – and you better facilitate their inclusion by listening to their requirements at every turn, or else you won't get asked back again. By constantly asking yourself 'Are they with me and have they got this?', you'll be forced to make theatre that's entertaining.

It's your job.

DEVISING IS NOT WRITING

Now you have begun making your show, you will start to create material/content and, for the most part, this will live in a space called *devising*. It looks like improvisation, but it's more anchored in creating a world based on your discussion.

Devising is about generating content, and writing is about taking this content and crafting it into a plot for the audience. They really are separate processes and it will pay you dividends early on to think of them as such. In fact, I'd go as far to say it may release some pressure from within the rehearsal room.

Yes, some of the things that you generate may be directly transcribed into the script, but that's rare; ultimately you will have to sit at a computer, jostle and filter it all through the act of writing. During the process of sculpting the devised material, the writer in you must take over and serve the gods of story, world, text, intention, objectives and plot. You will see-saw between the two and one can definitely feed the other, but you must always end up back at your keyboard to craft the content.

Now, I'm not saying that writing rules everything here – it's just going to be super-useful for you to acknowledge, early on, that the fun of making stuff will, at some point, have to be put through the more considered mechanism of scripting it into a coherent whole. Of course, they share the same space as they're both about making a show, but actors must create chaos with no live editing, and writers must mould it.

In a nutshell: devised material must earn its place in your piece – and the act of writing is its judge.

OFF-RAMPS

When you are in the devising stage, pop your head up occasionally in unexpected lands – for it's in these places where you can find hidden treasures rich for stealing and taking back home for your discussion.

I once made a show with a long-time collaborator of mine. We knew we wanted to make a music-based piece discussing a specific pop icon's influence over her fans, and that the show would live in the cabaret genre. After our initial 'Why now?' process, we started to think about fandom and in particular the fans of this artist. Next, we did our regular archaeological dig into the singer and her acolytes, whereupon we stumbled across a documentary about super-fans and were struck by how passionate they are.

This then led us to the tribute-act genre, which was when we discovered there used to be a particular venue in England that was devoted to acts who pay tribute to an artist by recreating their look and style, usually referred to as 'the tribute act'. The ideas were now coming thick and fast and, to cut a long story short, after looking at the private lives of tribute acts and their love of the main act, we created an act (using the artist's music) that tributes her *fans*. See? We subverted the expectations of the audience who thought they'd come to see a tribute act, but instead got a tribute to themselves – the fans.

It was a happy accident, but we just kept going – picking at it and getting lost (on purpose), because we always knew we were anchored to the shore by way of our initial research.

What did we want to discuss? Adulation, worship, religion and cults. And how did we get there? By following our idea up (unexpected) off-ramps.

STRUCTURE

Focusing on structure for a moment, I'm a fan of theatre that for the most part runs in regular time or at least with a linear plot. I'm also of the mind that unjustified scene changes can drop the energy of your piece and be a major distraction from the experience itself.

Having spent many rehearsals trying to direct a production with a scripted scene change, desperate not to lose any of the play's rhythms, I know it to be a mammoth task. When theatre is all about atmosphere and the audience's imagination is so fragile, we must interrogate why we suddenly drop it on the floor by stopping everything. Yes, you can play some fancy music and treat scene changes as a piece of dance, but they're just window dressing.

What's the solution? See if you can change scenes (places or time) without anyone noticing until after it's happened, and interrogate your plot's timeline. Ask why are you going to change momentum there? Why are you shifting from day to night? Because it's the evening? Great. Why does the plot require it to be night-time? Is it dramatically useful or is it just something you thought might be interesting?

The harder, less travelled, but more interesting path is to silently push through rather than announce a change. It may be unconventional, but I'd argue it's more theatrical.

INTERVALS
ARE OVER

Traditional theatre tends to comprise of two acts with an interval, and nowadays the interval seems to exist for two reasons. The first being the noble quest of the playwright needing to tell a long-form story, thus the insertion of a comfort break. The second being the theatre's objective of increasing their bar sales which, although less noble, is an equally important objective.

It's useful to note, though, that intervals seem to be dying out, which I believe to be a symptom of poorer artists making theatre to fit their economic limitations and – I suspect – the audience preferring to watch a kick-ass, ninety-minute show rather than a 130-minute marathon with 'some good bits' or a 'better second act'. It may also make economic sense for some venues to present shorter shows to allow them to host two events a night and double their ticket (and bar) sales.

So it seems we are now running towards having more one-act plays, with some commercial theatres still requiring two. The dream, of course, is for you to create a one-act show and then have some savvy producer invest in making it into a two-act one.

ADMIN

Whilst we are discussing the making of theatre, it's useful at this stage to briefly address the administrative side of our profession as it will always raise its head – no matter what stage you are at.

I hate admin, but I do like being organised, and knowing where everything resides is very important to me. Administration is the tool that I use to make this possible.

Running a production where everyone feels valued and secure is key to my ethos, and the formality of admin exists to support that whilst the show enters the chaotic side of the creative process. It's also intrinsically linked to my professional acumen, reputation and the image that I project. I'm not going to show you how to do it, but I do offer a warning: if you want to run a competent, tight ship, admin needs to be at the heart of it.

Tame and utilise the 'admin demon' and you'll have a room full of nourished and happy artists ready to risk their lives for you.

PRESERVE PERFORMANCE ART

14

I find performance art an interesting alternative to theatre, and although they share the same air, I believe them to be quite separate entities – and for good reason.

In its truest form, performance art raises questions and rarely seeks to provide any answers. It's not interested in looking after its audience; only seeking to maybe provoke them and then walk away. Theatre (and I mean straight-up live performance with a plot), wants to be understood in some way, shape or form.

I raise this thought as I think some theatremakers are using performance art in theatre spaces, or at least attempting to. Now, I'm always up for experimentation, but I think where it's presented is absolutely key. If it's in a gallery, museum, maybe a cabaret or an unconventional space, setting or event, then you may have more leeway to experiment with it, but if you're in a more regular theatre setting, remain mindful that the game is still very traditional and you may, at some point, look out to a sea of faces waiting for their inclusion in the event.

EDITING

A two-page scene is better than a six-page one.

But don't take my word for it – test the theory. Next time you are bored in the theatre or watching a film, it may mean that nothing is actually happening, or that the same thing is happening, or that everyone is speaking a lot, or that the same thing is happening, or everyone is speaking a lot, or that the same thing is happening, or everyone is speaking a lot. This script needs editing.

Think about your subplots for a moment. Can you bury them in fewer words? Make sure your characters are not saying what they 'want' or 'feel' too often. Sometimes it's needed, though; a character can just tell us plainly what they want, but maybe only let them say it after the audience has figured it out so we get to whisper 'I knew it!'

Use editing as the thing you must push against, to battle with and to conquer to get to your final destination. When you get editing right, you will discover what you really intended to discuss in a scene – and it feels amazing.

JEOPARDY

A delicious word of which I never tire.

Some people call it 'the stakes', but I prefer this precipice-inducing word. The idea that we don't know which way things will go, as the plot's momentum reveals itself.

Ask not what your characters can do for you, but what you can do *to* your characters.

INVISIBLE DIRECTION

The director (quite rightly) is the invisible, unsung hero. Yes, they may have the status of being at the 'top' of a very specific pyramid, but ultimately you'd be hard pushed to get anyone who's not in the know to define what a director does and the effect they have on a production.

I have directed many shows where I know that my choices are what the audience is experiencing – that it is was me who edited and interpreted the physical and verbal information that has been assembled to convey this live version of the writer or the company's play… and it'll never, ever be known by the audience because my choices are invisible. Only the other artists will be aware of my input – and even they will forget.

This is successful direction.

PLOT RULES

There is an idea that the plot of the play is the engine that drives the train. That the audience is considering what will happen next and the characters are revealing everything that's needed for them to understand and reconcile the plot of the play. I think this is true and we can all be carried along by this quite comfortably.

It is often described as 'What happens next?'

Check for yourself, though. Next time you are bored in the theatre or watching a film, it may be because the plot got lost up a side street somewhere and has left you behind.

I SAID, PLOT RULES

But you don't have to consider it straight away. It can come later.

You have your idea… and then the interrogation of that idea will reveal your discussion… followed (possibly) by you choosing a genre.

A story will then start to emerge in your head, which will need theatricalising – perhaps by way of devising – but it must all be put through the discipline of writing that obeys the rules of plotting.

BREAK A MOULD

When you're making theatre, other artists (of any discipline) may come to mind.

Observe a few that inspire you. Think about their careers, their artistic output and genre. Now study what it is that you like about them, and why them in particular. What is it that draws you in?

People I admire are unique and experimental and – for the most part – have shunted a genre along the road towards something new. They've reinvigorated a subsection of their genre that needed it, or created a new one.

Artists that live full, creative careers are always actively seeking to explore and break a genre, so I put it to you that whatever platform you settle on, find a way to push at its boundaries.

THE TICKET SALES

Theatre serves its audience. So, as a maker of theatre, you do too.

I think some of us have lost sight of our responsibility to the audience. A level of funding has (potentially) insulated any real risk away from the artist and placed it at the audience's feet, leaving them to witness some unfocused explorations, which I fear can lose those audiences along the way.

Sometimes, if we create work inside a financially sealed bubble, protected from any anxiety over ticket sales, we may lose sight that, honestly, sales are one of our main objectives.

DANCE

When I was at college, our dance teacher would sometimes be delayed in the morning, and so we would warm ourselves up to our latest CD and just get down with it.

We'd share moves we'd made up or seen in pop videos, and start choreographing our own routines – by the time our teacher turned up we'd be ready to rock. The reason? Dance. It creates euphoria. This is not news, but it's useful to remember when you are a bit stuck: put on some music and just dance.

The smiles will arrive, your body will wake up, and everyone's brain will also begin to… dance.

FLASHBACKS

The presentation of flashbacks or forwards on stage results from our addiction to the screen, not because they have justified their place in the theatremaker's toolkit as a proven, intellectual and useful storytelling device within the live act. I believe them (currently) to be intellectual ideas that seem fun in rehearsals, but have yet to be theatrically solved. They may be a useful tool on screen, but in the theatre they seem more like a side-step onto the stage at Pinewood, and not on to the theatrical one.

Now, I'm all for theatrical innovation, and the play *Constellations* by Nick Payne flirts with this displacement in time very well. I would argue, though, that each production I've seen of it still borrows from film by using a 'glitch' sound to signify that something has changed. But really the word-play inside *Constellations* is enough to dive into – we don't need the didactic soundtrack. Stephen Sondheim and James Lapine's musical *Sunday in the Park with George* moves *forward* one hundred years in Act Two and, as well as being bracing, our enjoyment is increased by having to join the dots by way of the prose – not by a shoe-horned cinematic device using flash choreography.

I'm not saying that theatrical flashbacks won't ever work, I just don't think they come from our theatrical skill set – they are currently being used as an intellectual add-on, not a genuine theatremaking tool.

Over to you.

TORTURE YOUR CHARACTERS

There's nothing more delicious for a writer than to torture a character/their audience.

I'm going to use a cinematic example for a moment from *The Green Mile*, a film based on a Stephen King novel, so pardon the side-step, but the rules still apply.

Eduard Delacroix, a convicted murderer on death row, is awaiting the electric chair. This form of execution back in the 1930s was pretty brutal, to say the least. The prisoner was strapped to a chair and a cap was placed on top of their shaved head that would deliver the killer-shock. In between the cap and the head, a wet sponge was inserted to ensure the electricity was conducted swiftly through the body – thus making it a brief experience for the onlooker and the recipient.

We really warm to Eduard Delacroix throughout the film because he cares for a small mouse, Mr Jingles. He feeds him and teaches him tricks, so this gives Delacroix – in the audience's eyes – a heart. In fact, I'd go as far to say that we actually forget that he's a convicted murderer. But of course, he must still be electrocuted.

Enter the rather delicious antagonist Percy Wetmore. Percy despises all convicted felons and is of the opinion that the electric chair is way too kind for any of them.

Delacroix's moment arrives. He is brought out and prepared for his execution. The straps are tightened and he's given the last rites, but Percy, whose one job it is to wet the sponge, fakes it, placing the sponge on to Delacroix's scalp – dry. Del doesn't die so quick. It's chaotic and barbaric to watch – and to make things worse, the chief warden knows that they must keep streaming the electricity through Delacroix's body as it's now the kindest thing to do.

The scene is awful, but super-powerful and the injustice of it all ups the jeopardy brilliantly because when Percy finally gets his comeuppance, it's the sweetest payoff.

Torture your characters and the possibilities will be electrifying.

MONEY IS NOTHING

I spoke to a Canadian theatremaker friend of mine recently and she said what she likes about the British theatre scene is that once we decide to make a show, we just begin – and think about the money later. I agree. But there also appears to be a received wisdom on the next step, and that is to apply for funding. Interesting. Is the possibility of doing this by yourself really no longer an option?

If you begin a project by asking 'I'll apply for funding in April and we'll start work in September', you may come up against a brick wall pretty quickly. Remember, your first instinct must be:

'I want to discuss this thing I see in the world on a stage.'

Next, you must pledge that by hook or by crook you will make this show. If you get a financial injection, great, but if you don't – you must still find a way. We need you.

ACADEMIC LANGUAGE

Academia is very useful for intellectual theories and the study of the arts. It is interesting to unpack prolific practitioners and their methods – but honestly, it has a very small stake in the making of something into a theatrical act, because the moment you transform yourself into a storytelling device, it's a state that only you can muster by way of your own imagination.

When your legs are wobbling and there are butterflies in your stomach, you will not be thinking about your super-objective, but about your next step. Yes, we can all hide away in rehearsals indulging ourselves in convincing 'techniques', but none of it exists in your performance. All you need is listening, projection, good self-management, and of course: a rich imagination.

Naturally, in rehearsals you will have discussions on psychology, sociology, anthropology, as well as your own lived experiences, and these may form a useful mash-up to enrich your imagination and solidify your approach, but your job as a theatremaker must be to listen, reply and serve the audience. You gain the confidence needed to do this by standing on a stage opposite other humans who are waiting for you to give something back to them.

For some reason, we are still made to believe that intellectual academic acting techniques lift up our trade, that they enable us somehow to better connect with our imaginations – but scholars come and go, strategies rise and fall, because every night the actor realises that the newest technique can't save them and the audience requires them on stage. Right now.

You're on.

DIRECTION WITHIN MOVEMENT

One thing I've noticed over the years is that if we don't understand the power of movement on stage we are missing an intrinsic superpower from our theatremaker's toolkit.

Movement is the visual language of theatre and it is as important (if not more important) to the production as the words themselves. You can literally change the plot or – at the very least – the intention of a moment through movement.

We also listen with our eyes.

MOVEMENT WITHIN DIALOGUE

There's a discussion (always ongoing) as to what action is on stage. Apparently, it's physical. Or at least a gesture. I suspect, however, that it can happen in prose too, so how did this 'physical-action-is-the-only-action' myth take hold?

Speeches/monologues in plays seem to be useful plot devices that freeze time and allow some breath, don't they? Whether they work in that particular play at that particular moment is for you to solve, but this blanket approach of 'everything must be *action*' (in its truest sense) seems like overkill. The audience is tuned into experiencing stories in many ways and will automatically switch over to whatever mode you need them to, as long as you haven't dropped their imagination on the floor.

If your prose is written in a poetic way that embellishes the character or story, surely you are okay to stop the world and get off for a period of reflection? Inaction can muster action, no?

I do believe, however, that you will be on borrowed time.

CREATE SPACES

You must learn to identify what you need to be able to create. I think environment is key.

Mix up your spaces by way of cafés, bars, theatres, cinemas and libraries, and try to hone the skill of knowing when you should stop working, walk away and find a new space. You don't have to take your computer or your journal with you everywhere you go, as it's enough for you just to travel with your ideas and go sit in a field, or somewhere just as radical.

Your brain will still be whirring away in the background.

INTERROGATION

It's useful to interrogate your topic by strength-testing your discussion. But how do you do this? By reading, watching and observing the absolute opposite of your idea. If you don't have a counteraction vibrating within your play, the work may appear as propaganda and, truthfully, will end up as a mere conduit for the information you've carefully selected.

Remember, you are not the only one who is right – you are flawed and full of misinformation. Remain mindful that your audience may have different opinions and that your job is not to change them, but to discuss and leave questions in the air. Theatricalise both sides of a discussion and people will flock to your door to understand each other's worlds.

SCI-FI

I have a playwright friend who is adamant that science fiction doesn't work on stage. Although I hate to admit it – I think they're right.

Of course, there's *been* sci-fi on stage, but apart from the deliciously silly and rather successful *Return to the Forbidden Planet*, there's not one that I can think of that has truly defined it. Some stage shows have flirted with it (*Rocky Horror* and… erm… *Little Shop of Horrors*); others have utilised the idea of robots and spaceships – but sci-fi and theatre still don't seem to work well together.

Prove my friend wrong?

THEATREMAKERS ARE DRAMATURGS

Dramaturgs tend to observe and then evaluate the shape, tone and potential impact of a piece of theatre. They'll more than likely make a contribution to the research phase and they may also be in the room acting as a dramatic judge.

Is this role required? Are dramaturgs a luxury for the wealthy? A necessary position? Do these skill sets really need to be farmed off to one individual? Does it *truthfully* need its own subsection? It's certainly had a renaissance of late.

Now, as far as I understand, when making a new piece it's my responsibility to do the research, strength-test it, filter it, write it up, look at the landscape, and then keep editing until I'm happy with the result. Of course, I will ping that over to a few trusted friends or members of my team, but I personally wish to be in charge of the discovery.

I'm a Theatreturg – and I love a treasure hunt.

DIRECTION IS...

INTERPRETATION

HUNTING

TRAILBLAZING

SKILFUL

SCULPTING

INTENSE

MAGIC

LEADERSHIP

POLITICS

STRESSFUL

FOUND

LEADERSHIP

FIXING

WATCHING

CRAFTING

EDITING

LISTENING

POSTER DESIGN

MANAGEMENT

STUDYING

ART

COLLABORATION

ATMOSPHERE

STRUCTURE

VISION

CAJOLING

CONTROL

ANALYSIS

CONSOLIDATION

INSTINCT

INTERROGATION

DEVISING

WRITING

HARD WORK

INSIGHT

COUNSELLING

DISCOVERED

ADHESION

ENCOURAGING

INVISIBLE

IMAGINATION

PREPARATION

PLUMBING

PROVOKING

MEETINGS

DIRECTION IS NOT...

TELLING
or
SHOWING

ACTING IS...

TIMELESS

ENERGY

SCARY   MOVEMENT   REBELLION

SILLY

FUNNY   WORDS

ART

DISCUSSION

VOICE   TIME   SPACE

PLAY

ENTERTAINMENT   LIFE-PAUSED

BODY   COLLABORATION   TRUST   MIMETIC

COMMUNICATION   LIFE-EXAGGERATED

STORYTELLING   CURATION

POWERFUL   INNOCENCE   CHILDLIKE

PRESENCE

NEEDED   POLITICAL   RIDICULOUS

UNDERSTANDING   REQUIRED   LISTENING

WATCHING   PREPARATION   PHILANTHROPIC

SINCERE   CONFIDENCE   INDULGENT

ENGAGEMENT   STRESSFUL

IMAGINATION   HARD WORK

INSIGHT

ACTING IS NOT...

THE LEARNING OF LINES

BLOCKING

'Blocking' is an awful, old-fashioned term. Direction must be discovered then crafted, so please jettison the word 'blocking' from our world immediately. Actors are not chess pieces and you are not choreographing a dance.

Find your direction based on the discussion of the play, the text and the other billion ideas in the room.

WHAT THE AUDIENCE SECRETLY WANTS

I've spoken before about the theatre's duty to entertain and to discuss the world we live in, as I believe the best live art to be the one that picks our world apart and gives everyone who witnesses it an opportunity to rebuild it as they see fit, after watching some truths be played out in front of them.

The genre of stand-up comedy seems to be the most concentrated example of this, as every word counts and comedians know that when they get a rich laugh it's because they've spoken a truth; albeit through a joke. But how can we cultivate this approach?

By *creatively* presenting the things that we're not always allowed to say openly; and maybe going into areas we don't want to and by remaining in service to the audience's thirst for truth, I believe we can raise our game and keep theatre honest; an arena for truthful discussion.

Check out the work of Hannah Gadsby, Richard Pryor, George Carlin, Victoria Wood, Joyce Grenfell or Lenny Bruce to witness some truth-telling through performance. Lenny Bruce's act was considered so controversial he actually had the cops attend his act, ready to arrest him if he told too many truths.

WHAT THE AUDIENCE NEEDS

The act of theatre undoes itself if it does not also dissect its own politics at some point, and the only way I can represent my theory is to use the political chasms that have emerged in the UK since the EU Referendum in 2016.

In Great Britain we seem to be using divisive language more and more these days by calling each other 'The Left', 'The Right', 'Remoaners' or 'Gammons'. This divide (in some settings) – albeit in families, friends or even households – is quite palpable.

Essentially, though, we all want the same things: love, warmth, respect, a home, family, a job, etc. The realistic, more believable political divide seems to be about how the government is run – the divvying up of the money – and whether it represents us personally. Sometimes our view is in and sometimes it is out, but the wheel always turns back the other way at some point.

So let's imagine for a moment you are making a show about leaving the European Union; now let's say you were against the idea and that your show has this discussion inside it. I put it to you, however, that if you are a real public servant you must also include the counter-argument in favour of leaving the EU and both 'sides' must also be held to ransom.

How does this make you feel? Uncomfortable? Great. That's just anxiety, so leap past that and test the theory that if you do discuss everyone's views and nuance the debate, you are fully equipped to potentially join people together by way of a discussion. Now, isn't that worth it?

AVOID THE CINEMA

I don't mean to literally avoid the cinema, as I adore it. No – what I mean is: avoid replicating the conventions of film on the stage.

There are a few differences between the two mediums. Film is image, tech, words, movement, planning, doctoring, editing and permanence. Theatre is image, metaphor, words, movement, poetry and liveness. It is the execution of organic parts in a particular order to create a world that executes a plot. A film is a director's vision and the theatre is the actor's imagination being played out.

See film not as something to copy but as your offspring. You enjoy it on occasion because of its fancy tech, but walk away confident knowing that you work in the theatre and that it gave birth to film.

YOUR LIFE ON STAGE?

Should your life be on the stage? If you think 'Yes, absolutely' – return to 'Why now?'

First, you must speak to the world you live in and, second, you must bring something new to the genre that hasn't been seen before – or at least not for a long time. You may not achieve this, but it's enough to ask the questions, and trust me – something will shift.

We all secretly want world domination, right? A TV commission based on our idea, a film, a franchise or (at the very least) the chance of it; because then you will be in a financial position to make new theatre. But this success may only be achieved once you have stirred and conquered the audience's apathy by giving them what they want in a way they never expected.

Your life on stage? Why?

ELECTRONIC SOUND

Electronic sound in the theatre is still a new thing that I don't think we've quite tamed. Now, I'm not talking about cabaret, performance art or comedy here. No, I'm talking about straight plays – and possibly musicals to some extent – that have begun to use electronic sound to create an atmosphere in a scene with dialogue – in short: soundtracking a live show. This is film. Yes, here I go again.

Several elements of theatremaking have ballooned over the years in the spirit of experimentation (sound being one of them), and I'd argue that this is directly related to the unchecked influence of the cinema. The orchestration of a dramatic scene by way of sound design reveals your true intention which is somehow to manipulate the audience. But you're replicating the cinematic experience and removing the live one.* In short: electronic soundscapes must be measured and held to the same standard as everything else you add into your show. Like a prop, it must earn its place by offering something meaningful to the live experience and not live as its own tricksy, intellect-based add-on.

Now, I'm not saying all sound designers must be sacked or we should have fewer sound designers. What I'm saying is that we (the theatremakers) must make sure we have a hand in what, how and when something goes into our work. We should ask ourselves 'Is this required?' and 'What is it adding?', because if we're not careful, we may be erecting a sound barrier that actually removes the audience's organic freedom to feel what they want. The theatre is not a film.

Last thought: If you feel you have to end your play on a deep bass 'boom', you've gone to the bad place. This 'doom' belongs on *Transformers* and not in the theatre.

God, I'm old.

---

* Actors: defend your job to create atmosphere by way of your live decisions as this mission creep could slowly erode your instinct and autonomy.

PROTAGONISTS

How-to books sometimes pedal a yarn that you must only have one protagonist. This is archaic and needs to be shelved. Why? Because we have evolved. And so has the audience. We are now very sophisticated listeners and can quite easily handle multi-layered drama and no longer need to be pointed in one direction. Of course, you can still use one protagonist, but remember it's possible to make ensemble-based theatre.

I don't need to prove this here for you today. Keep your eyes and ears peeled and you'll start to spot dual-protagonist stories, and they've always been there. You may not approve, but they exist and are just as successful.

PLAY

There was a controversial moment in *Jerusalem* by Jez Butterworth when Mark Rylance, for a very brief second, looked out at the audience, and acknowledged we were here too. It was electrifying. We were still watching the character, but there was something remarkable going on underneath all of it; like an acknowledgment from Mark that this was all a game and that Rooster (the 'character') was also about to do something mischievous.

Watching theatre is hard work and so providing light relief from time to time is a gift. It releases the pressure cooker and gives everyone some time out. Make your show fun, no matter what. Bring some joy and laughter to a drama and you'll win. Comedy, tragedy, tears – they all swim in the same pool. Dive in.

DEEP DISCUSSIONS

I've spoken before about the discussion of your piece and that it is important to be open to contrary points of view. If you create theatre that merely underlines your own personal politics, only the people you agree with will come and see your show, because you're treating the stage as your soapbox. Whereas a true discussion-based piece is dynamic, layered and has multiple viewpoints.

Now, I want you to think about the middle ground for a moment, whereby two sides of an argument are briefly in agreement. This is also the area where the deepest conflict and drama can lie. For instance, remember our Charlie Chaplin life-story show? It was going to discuss how women were silenced off-camera as well as on. Well, the middle-ground conflict could manifest as a character.

Meet Harold…

Harold is a cameraman on Chaplin's silent movies. He has worked in film for about ten years and doesn't want things to change, even though sound is now being introduced across the industry. His daughter, Sally, works on the films as an actress. She wants talkies to happen so she can finally be heard. She's an amazing singer and Harold knows that if the public hear her sing she could be a star – but the silent movies are where he makes his living…

Do you see where I'm going? Find the middle ground in your discussion and you will discover some lovely micro-tensions to torture your characters/audience with.

TREASURE HUNTS

Terrestrial TV and streaming services are – past, present and future – obsessed with the crime genre. There are thousands and thousands of episodic shows all using the same plot device, which is basically the 'hunt for a treasure' of some sort. It seems the public loves a mystery. This is useful to note as I'm convinced that when the audience is asking 'What will happen next?', we have an opportunity to trick them and bury some fake treasures.

In your show, consider concealing some of your valuable plot points because when the audience do find something that may finally solve the mystery – oh, the euphoria! (Which leads to applause and probably more ticket sales.)

THERE ARE NO FORMULAS

Throughout your career, you will hear actors, directors, producers and writers telling you their Top Ten ways to make theatre (me included).

Listen to them. Steal what you agree with, and disregard what you don't, because although they won't directly help you make your show – they may enable it.

Take what feels truthful and abandon the rest.

EXPOSITION BAD?

Exposition is a tricky one to pin down. One theory is that bad exposition is characters overtalking about stuff that's happened offstage that's not relevant to the actual plot on the stage. I'm not sure if that's always true, though, as we can't totally divine what information some people require or what they will do with it, as everyone listens and interprets things differently, no?

Take a song, for instance. Full of exposition – but the audience lets it wash over them and they do their own maths. Yes, it's musicalised – but that's kinda my point: find a vehicle for the important information that has made it through your edit, that's furthering your plot and related to your discussion, and I reckon you will dodge the bad exposition landmine.

Perhaps introducing a TV/radio/phone element, a letter arriving, someone's journal being discovered, finding an old picture, a dead body or an object will also give your 'information' an anchor, a place in your plot and keep it in the world of your piece.

KNOW THE WHOLE PLOT

This may be an obvious thing to say, but seriously, every actor must know the whole world of the show. If you don't, you will be seen as a guest star, and the audience will pick up on it. Plays are political acts; you don't want to appear halfway through a revolution not knowing the politics but still expecting to lead.

THEATREMAKER LOSES CONTROL

Understand that the bigger the infrastructure you find yourself in, the less control you have. The more successful your show is, the more likely an external producer might be brought in, at which point you could start to lose some autonomy. Remain active and present.

RABBIT HOLES

When you are researching and devising, you will come across what are called 'rabbit holes', moments when the show seems to veer off-piste. This is good. Allow it to happen.

Maybe take the audience where you're going – and remember: every rabbit hole always leads back to the surface.

USE MUSIC

Music is a fundamental part of my life. It can conjure images, my past, an atmosphere; it stirs my emotions and can even send me to sleep.

As you are building your project, make a playlist that will instruct your streaming service to send you suggestions. If you don't use an online provider for your music, make a list of words that best describes the show you are making, go to YouTube and put the word 'music' on the end of one of your words; e.g. political music, children's music, forgotten music from the thirties – someone somewhere will have compiled something, believe me.

Soak it all up and shift over any little gems that appear to your main show's playlist. You'll be surprised how you'll find an artist from a different era who's made something that's absolutely what you require.

CONJURE THE PRODUCTION

This is an intellectual concept and it's something that can't technically be taught; it has the same airy-intention of 'find a direction'. I'll get into it more later in the next chapter about making your production, but it's useful to note now as the line between the show and the production is very thin.

Every aspect of the production must be conjured in line with the spirit of the play (the discussion). The font, the music, the posters, the costumes – all of it. In short: sculpt your show.

PREVIEWS AND PRESS

Previews are theatrical acts inside the production of theatre. They are the internal theatre of theatre producers, venues and press.

We are led to believe that everything rests on these preview and press nights. I think this to be intellectual hooey. They now feel more like a historical re-enactment rather than a twenty-first-century-specific marketing tactic – especially as the rebalancing of the critic's role, the diminishing profiles of the mainstream media and the seismic effects of social media are becoming evident. It seems the old ways may actually be over.

I'm not advocating that press nights should be removed – far from it. Just that we see them for what they are: a lot of extraneous theatrical hot air that performers must be protected from.

RECORDING YOUR SHOW

If you've made an original piece, you are allowed to document it. Still, remember to get everyone's permission, and state it's for archival purposes only. If the piece is written by someone else, you will need their permission, and that may incur costs – especially if a publisher or agent is involved.

Think about sound when filming in a theatre because most of the time it translates badly. If your show includes music and microphones, get some professional advice. The usual way is to take the sound straight from the desk, but this can create an insular quality so it may need mixing in post-production with the room's actual sound. Seek advice.

Also, avoid filming it in secret. It will look like it's filmed in secret and will be of questionable quality. Only amateurs film shows illegally. The rules are there to protect other artists. Follow them.

FLYERING

We'll get into marketing later, but as I mentioned before, our all-encompassing skill set overlaps at every turn – so a quick thought about flyering.

I've noted that when performing in a festival, many artists (Edinburgh especially) pay people to flyer for them. I think this is a great idea. Of course, you must have flyers in your bag, but if you can budget for a few people to flyer for you, you will thank the day you did, as you sit drinking tea in bed, three hours before your show goes up.

PLAY FORMATS

Years ago the playwright would try to direct the actor, or (god forbid), the whole play by way of endless stage directions – inadvertently sucking out all the energy of their own work. Thankfully those days are (mostly) over.

Dialogue must be your priority, avoid directing it and make sure the reader/performer understands you.

THREE-STAR REVIEWS

Three-star reviews – don't publish them. They're not useful. Four or five stars only.

If they're from a prolific publication then sure, grab some useful pull-quotes, but other than that – don't use the three-star grading on your marketing.

WRITING COMPETITIONS

If you have a script on the shelf, should you enter it into a writing competition? They are a strange beast and I only enter them if the challenge interests me and they have a decent financial reward or a guaranteed production at the end of it. My next step will be to investigate the judges and see if I rate them. If, after all of this, I have an idea I want to explore – then maybe I'll do it.

Never write just for the possibility of winning a fee because there are quicker ways to end your love for writing.

FEEDBACK QUESTIONS

There's a lovely analogy that a painter does not ask the onlooker where they think the paintbrush should go next. Whilst the sentiment of this is useful to remember, as theatremakers, our income is based on a successful manipulation of the audience experience, so I do advise a sharing of new material at some point to expose your work to some feedback. But, after your sharing, ask specific questions – as there is such a thing as unuseful feedback, which usually begins with one of these two sentences:

'I would have done this…'
'I think you should have…'

Although well-meaning, they are essentially based on other people's desires, what they would have done had they made your show, and you must preserve your version.

Here are a few questions I've inherited over the years that I've found to be useful that encourage the onlooker to become a little more specific in their interpretation:

'What have I created?'
'Can you describe back what you just watched?'
'What did you want more/less of?'
'Where would you expect this to be staged?'
'What would you call this play?'
'Was there anything you didn't understand?'

There may be confusion in the feedback session as you will be (in some ways) restraining other people's theatremaking politics, but allow it to happen. Protect your show.

PART 2

MAKING A
PRODUCTION

The production – the process of manufacturing a show – is the invisible thing you manage that facilitates the show's physical manifestation. It nurtures it, binds and elevates everything into existence – thus giving birth to the show, which is the displaying of dramaturgical decisions by way of a performance. The show can technically exist without the production (enact the words and actions in front of an audience), but the production of a show is what raises it up to be an event.

In some ways, I think the production of a show is an indefinable thing; first it must be curated in your head, and then created by some very careful decision-making.

And it never stops, until the rather strange day when it does. The last night and definitely the morning after a show must be one of the most mind-altering moments in our careers. Trying to smile sweetly in the bar whilst wondering if you steered the production correctly is bizarre; especially knowing that tomorrow – now that the showing is over – you must pick over its embers, pack it all away and then reflect on the union between the show and the production.

The next sixty thoughts concentrate on the micro-stresses you might encounter as your show demands a production that is a true representation of its parts, whilst you enable it to become a streamlined and successful live moment.

SET SERVES PLOT

Everything must be in service to the discussion of the piece.
Make a note of that: in service.

Nowadays there seem to be two choices of set designs:
literal and metaphorical. There are no doubt many other
important micro-terminologies that can be used, but by
using this simple two-sided labelling system for a moment
it's easier for me to offer up my next thought.

If a set is literal and your money is everlasting, your designer
will more than likely aim for absolute authenticity on stage.
They may spend weeks sourcing the right tap from Poland
for your Second World War play. Why? Because they can.
Now I imagine you to be thinking: 'Russell is going to pull
this ideology down.' Well – not this time. Some people really
want to see these types of intricate designs on stage, and I
for one always marvel at a house, a horse or a boat on stage.
It's totally obscene and not needed at all, but it gives us all
a sugar hit and, as ticket-buyers, we feel like we're being
served. A *theatrical* version of a house, a horse or a boat on
stage would be more fun, though – more theatre, no? (Joey,
the horse in *War Horse*, is the most perfect illusion.)

Metaphorical sets are generally an ambiguous gesture to
a place or a element within the play. This is what I believe
theatre sets should really be. Why? Because theatre isn't real
life and it's not film. If you have everything down to the last
detail, it means there's been little in the way of tension for
you to push against or contain your choices. In fact, how
about starting with no set and build up?

All this aside – the set designer, whilst having their own
adventure, must remain anchored in service to the piece.
If your play is set in a room and you don't need the walls –
find a reason to put them up before you do.

SELL TICKETS

I may come across as an anti-establishment anarchist, which I am sometimes, but I am also a capitalist at heart who wants to make a living out of their business by selling tickets. But how do I do this?

Well, friends and family sales are baked in. Other theatremakers are probably a given too. Social media is very important – and I will talk about that later on – but there is a plethora of alternative ways to sell tickets, and I have found that, by tapping into my creativity, I come up with fresh strategies to make it happen.

In the past I have looked at charities, Wikipedia pages, fan-sites, or even fine artists that may want to promote their work by partnering with me. I once contacted a GIF designer who was making art related to my subject and she allowed me to share them under my show's umbrella for free, even after I offered to pay her. We had quite a big fan base online who in turn latched onto her artwork, thus nourishing her profile. What else you got?

STAGING
IS NOT ENOUGH

I have come away from shows in the past and thought that
they were staged very well, but they lacked life. After further
contemplation I realised that the shows had been blocked.
That awful, old fashioned, insipid technique that is basically
the overmanagement of everything by way of choreography
masquerading as direction. Blocking can be seen inside the
Disneyfication of musicals, the facsimiles of plays, and it's
all born from the trade's unflinching attempt to commodify
the theatrical experience.

But how can we resist overchoreographing a show within
an inch of its life? By way of actors. The theatre is theirs,
and the audience have come to see them live out a life, so
give them back some territory. Of course, the direction
must exist every night, but there has to be some air for
spontaneity. It goes back to that thought about sound. No
one person, other than the actor, must – or can – truly drive
the rhythms of the show by their live decisions.

If you're wincing at that statement you are probably a
director, producer or teacher; I'm here to tell you – as
someone who wears multiple hats – we are overmanaging
our actors, stunting their skills, or worse – removing them
all together by co-opting their autonomy and attempting to
preside over every inch of the live experience. The theatre
belongs to them, not us. Everyone else is a mere footman,
door opener, cushion plumper, and if you don't take glee
by secretly knowing it's you that facilitates their process, get
out of the dark and on to the stage; it's probably where you
secretly wish to be.

Yes, I know theatre is collaborative, and everyone is needed,
but dial it back because nothing must invade the air created
by the performer.

MORE INTERROGATION

What does everything mean?

ACTOR NEEDED

We seek an artist, a wordsmith and a storyteller; a fool with a humble spirit who possesses a resonant voice, who can conjure size from within their soul by drawing upon a deep connection with their imagination.

YOUR RUNNING TIME

You must serve the running time of your show. If you have a sixty-minute slot and you run over, it means you're either not a strong enough editor – or you've gone to the bad place where nothing exists except you and your show. If you don't serve the running time there will be a very frustrated venue manager tapping a toe somewhere or, worse still, another theatremaker waiting to get into the space with their important life-changing work of art. And what about your audience who thought it was a sixty-minute show?

Yes, I know – cutting stuff out is hard, but it means you may have made an error booking your show into this particular timeslot in the first place and probably need a rethink.

Make a fifty-five-minute show, and any stress and anxiety that has built up around any time restrictions will be removed – and everyone will enjoy the five-minute wiggle room. Honour the deal.

ACTORS CONTROL EVERYTHING

I'm very much of the mind that the theatre is the actors. Did you get that message yet? You will hear this a lot through various quotes – but is it really true? Not as far as actors are concerned it isn't.

This is very sad and if you wanted to place blame anywhere it's probably best to lay it at the actors' feet as they have been more than happy to give up some territory in exchange for asking others to navigate them through an impossible system that has eroded their value. There are so many firewalls erected these days between the audience and the actor, and there's only one person that can keep that obstruction in check: the actor. How? By removing some of these firewalls and then allowing only the useful, the more honourable collaborators into the game.

We are now living in the aftermath of the catastrophic Covid shutdowns of 2020–21, and it is going to be very interesting to see how performers wrestle with this new land. I hope that right now they are asking: 'Was I genuinely happy with everything the way it was before and who do I trust with my career now?'

CAST PROPERLY

Casting is a trick. It's technical knowledge, blended with an instinct for art.

For me, the actor I always hope to cast is a keen storyteller and an avid wordsmith. The true actor knows they must first serve the piece, which in turn will evolve to them becoming a verbally dexterous conduit for the writing. They will be aware of the possibility of language and the power of live performance. I seek spirit, humility and dexterity; in short – an open soul. But how do you cast for that? I don't know the magic formula, but it's enough to identify what you truly desire, and then go beyond what you initially think you want.

DON'T JUST ACCEPT DIRECTORS

69

Anyone can call themselves an actor, writer, producer or director. That's the point of theatre: it's humans performing in front of other humans and there never will be (nor should there be) a verification tick required before one can be any of the above. But. The professional versions of these jobs come with a set of expectations and responsibilities.

Take directors, for example: how can you check someone's credentials in this area? How do you verify that they can actually direct? Well, first, don't presume they can just because they call themselves a director. Meet them, find out what work they've made, check reviews, and talk to other people who have worked with them. Also, have them come and do a short session with you as part of the interview (buy them lunch/coffee or pay for their travel). Ask whose work they admire, favourite films, writers, etc. All of this will give you an idea of whether or not you have chemistry. Many of us work together in this trade just because we are artists, but it soon becomes awkward once we realise the relationship is lacking the artistic pizzazz required actually to make work.

Now if you're a performer that's looking for a director and you slightly shudder when I suggest that you check out a director's credentials, you are already playing the lowly actor-slave in an old-fashioned hierarchy. Get rid of it immediately. The mechanic and the driver must work together to get the car on the road.

SCHEDULES

I have learned that a sixty-minute, fully formed play will need, at the very least, three weeks in a rehearsal room. This is putting aside casting, meetings, production, marketing, etc.

Make sure you schedule your days smartly and be confident enough to have some time off. Offer snacks, games if you like, warm-ups if required. Keep to it, but also respond organically. Sometimes you can let people go early or arrive later. Invite a daily structured freedom into the room – rehearsals should also be fun and relaxed, even though you still require specific results.

Example:

9:15 a.m.	Producer/Director arrives to set up
9:45 a.m.	Actors called for coffee and chat
10:15 a.m.	Session One
11:45 a.m.	Comfort break
12 p.m.	Session Two
1:30 p.m.	Lunch
2:30 p.m.	Session Three
4 p.m.	Comfort break
4:30 p.m.	Session Four
5:45 p.m.	Reflection
6 p.m.	Finish

AVOID OVERPLANNING

Although your timetable holds you all together, it's not an immovable feast. If you need to change it then do so, but still aim to keep a structure to the day with some expected outcomes. When I talk about a results-based system, what I mean is that you don't have to have too many specific expectations on what you must achieve each day, because this process is really like cooking – you have all of your ingredients and each one needs to be heated at different times by a different method, ready for consuming. If your director is worth their salt, this will be second nature to them.

YOU'RE POWERLESS

When the curtain rises, if you are not the actor, you are now just a powerless onlooker waiting for the performer to make the next decision. This is how it should be. If you're the director, you hope they execute what you have taken months to craft; and if you're the producer you can but use every trick in the book to sell the tickets. If you are both, make sure you compartmentalise the two roles. If you're everyone else, you can't do anything else except wait for your cue to execute your job. That cue comes from the actor, because there's no one more powerful than the actor during showtime – no matter the assertions from the rest of us.

IS IT THEATRE?

This thought is linked to choosing the medium that suits you and your discussion/show. It could be that the stage is now not the place for your work, and that it might be better served on film, radio or as an online short. Allow this thinking into your practice and you might find some much-needed liberation and develop a new skill set for the future. Radio is a soundscape, and film is a highly curated filmmaker's vision. Theatre is a live, visual medium built on illusion that always needs a performer present.

AUTEURS

74

The auteur concept returns to the theatrical canon every so often. It's no one special because technically, we are all auteurs – but the category creates enough of a buzz and keeps the chattering classes buying a ticket and their over-priced thimble of Sauvignon.

A director may one day be unlucky enough to receive this poisoned chalice, at which point they have two choices: either they start believing the hype and think that they can make '*Hamlet* on the *Titanic*'* work – or they can smile sweetly, return back to their studio and wait for the marketing departments to calm down – which is the more preferable outcome. Auteurs, like the winner of a TV singing competition, will more than likely live a short professional life if they too believe they are a master of the art and forget that they are a student of the audience.

* '*Hamlet* on the *Titanic*' would probably sell. Damn it.

TRIGGER ME

Bring down the world and rebuild it on the stage every night, and you'll have a queue of people around the block crying out for some unplanned chaos in their theatres and their lives.

THE FUN STUFF

The fun stuff is things like posters, names, announcements, and social-media accounts. Whilst we can find a sense of productivity in creating these, do you really need a Twitter account for every show you make? I suggest that you, as the professional you are, seek a one-voice-only social-media account that is a confident platform for all your work. An ongoing foghorn that creates a following based on your artistic output – not your fleeting artistic projects. If you have a global, long-running hit then that's a whole different thing but, in the meantime, take a load off your shoulders and create one rich voice that demonstrates your eclectic career rather than spreading it out over too many apps.

PS: Avoid the phrase 'delighted to announce' because everyone's saying it. What else you got?

POSTERS

Talking of the fun stuff…

Let me tell you about a journey I recently went on with a poster designer. In 2017, I knew I wanted to make a piece based on the American politician Bobby Kennedy. I had created a few bits of material, but nothing solid and so it was then that I thought I was ready to work with a designer to at least give me an image to worship. I met with an artist I knew from another project and whose work I admired. We had an exchange of emails whereby I sent him some visual references and we began to share an online mood board. More time passed and then we finally had a face-to-face meeting as I felt I had reached the point where I didn't know what I wanted but would know when I saw it. After that, he went away and then presented something back to me – which fired me up even further. I was then able to sling my research and desires at his idea and a poster was born. It was collaborative, but most of all – it's now part of the show's life-force.

AFTER YOUR FAMILY HAS LEFT

I spoke before about your family and friends being in your first wave of ticket sales and how, after they have seen the show and have all left, you will be in a very different state of being.

This is the truest experience of your actual job and it's based in solitude. It is, to my mind, the most humbling moment for a theatremaker: to entertain people you don't know, who are paying you to do it.

AUTEURS #2

No profession should hijack a show.

THE SADDEST THING SOMEONE SAID

...was when a fellow theatremaker uttered the following: 'In some ways it doesn't matter if I sell a ticket.' My eyebrows raised, but then lowered swiftly when I remembered this person had had a handsomely funded career. Of course, it did matter a few years later when their show didn't sell so well, but their original statement was still very striking to me and, bizarrely, I actually felt endorsed – I am a very happy ticket-slave.

There was once a very famous producer who used to put on big shows, but in the past ten years they've stopped making original content. Why? Because after three or four successes they only had flops. Why? Because they could suddenly do anything they wanted and what they wanted was no longer in tune with what the world wanted. How did this happen? No risk. They have huge amounts of cash in their bank which presents a thousand options. How numbing.

I am a humble busker on the stage, holding out his hat, hoping for the coins to be thrown at me, and that if that doesn't happen I will go away and do some serious homework – hopefully emerging as a better artist. My priority is to sell tickets and, if I don't have this concern, I believe I will run into the danger of having part of my producer radar stunted and my entrepreneurial skills diminished.

THE ZEITGEIST

Listen carefully and your muse (the zeitgeist) will tell you
what it wants next. This may be by way of applause,
reviews, popular TV, what's flopping at the cinema, which
actors are big now and who has fallen out of favour. It could
be through politics, food, fashion, music, ticket sales, social
habits, history or news.

These are the things you must learn to tune into because
therein lies your next show.

TIME OFF

I am a firm believer in 'slow and steady wins the race'. I think it was the actress Lily Tomlin who said that 'The trouble with the rat race is that even if you win, you're still a rat.' She was onto something.

If you've reached a point whereby you can no longer create, back off – and don't feel guilty about it. Remember it's just taking some time off, not time out. Go watch a film in a cinema you've never been to or go to a gallery. Invest in two nights in a new city – whatever you need, just do it. Anything to get you out of your funk. Dance, watch trash TV, make a pizza, or go on a boat trip to get some perspective. It's all valid because this period is absolutely part of your journey.

Lean in.

ELECTRONICA

Electronica has one foot deeply embedded in the experimental and avant-garde, and I believe it to be a very useful partner to theatre's left-field spirit. Don't get it confused with electro or electronic dance music. Do some research into the origins of the genre and find the pioneers. Listen to them. Programme your music-streaming service to send you suggestions based on your tastes and this will only enrich your work and take you into off-ramps you'd never dreamed of.

TALKS

A quick off-ramp for you…

In Thought #4 we spoke about identifying the discussion within your piece, and in #52 you listed some words that described the world you are creating. Well, there are hundreds of online talks by scholars, experts and aficionados, and I bet you'll find one linked to your investigations that will inspire some new content.

BIOGRAPHIES

If you are making a show about someone prolific, your first
port of call may be their biography. This is a natural first
step, but think of it as surface research only – you must go
to the next level at some point. Your job is to theatricalise
that life, not fastidiously represent someone else's book
on stage. Also check if this person's life is actually in the
public domain and is considered 'fair game'. Each country
will have their own interpretation of what is considered
public domain, so do some deep research. The internet
will more than likely supply you with your answers; failing
that, contact other artists who have produced shows based
on prolific people in the country you are making the work.
If you can afford it or know someone who knows one, an
entertainment lawyer could also prove useful.

In my experience, it's about how you frame your show
and that it's made clear that no one from their camp has
endorsed it, but do your homework.

YOUR MIRROR PRODUCTION

At times you will find that as soon as you begin your new project, you discover that someone somewhere will be making something very similar on film or even for theatre. Don't panic. I've had it several times and I just chalk it up to another artist divining the world in the same way as me, but it's highly unlikely that they'll be entering the material from the same point. That said, it's important to do your research on past or upcoming productions. There's always something on your topic – I guarantee you; it could be in poetry, paintings, or an article. It's just a case of finding it.

My dance teacher used to say, 'There's no such thing as an original dance move.' Obviously this used to infuriate me as I always approached my choreography as if I was reinventing the wheel (a perfect strategy, by the way), but I now know what he meant: there's only so many ways the human body can move, but that it's the way you reconfigure them that's key. Your interrogation and interpretation (the production), are individual and if you bend a genre, you've already left the rest behind.

87 LET IT SOAK

I've spoken about this before, but I'm raising it again as it also applies to the schematics of production. If you have an idea but are unsure of how to execute it, sometimes the best thing is to acknowledge it and leave it on the shelf. If it has value, your instinct will bring it back to you. It will prod you at some point and say, 'Hey, it's time.'

APPLAUSE EARS

Have you ever been in a theatre and about five minutes before showtime, the audience suddenly goes quiet for no reason? I know exactly when this is about to happen, and it's fascinating to study. There's a minute shift in the volume of the room and suddenly it's as if something has happened – or is about to.

As a theatremaker, you must be finely tuned to the sound of applause as it tells you everything you need to know. For instance, when the lights go down and the audience applauds, it signifies they're up for it. Euphoria is present. If there is a polite, muted applause after Act One, it's the audience behaving the way they think they should. If it's rapturous, they are very, very grateful and the excitement of Act Two will be palpable. If at the end of your show the audience unanimously rises to their feet, it's honest and you have a hit on your hands. If there is a peppered standing ovation, it's a mix of people who stand at every show and others who feel they should – or just people who want to see the actors bow.

SINGING ALONG

I'll never forget when a musical based on a famous pop artist's life put up a sign in the foyer asking the audience not to sing along. How insulting to their audience. This is why they had come; it's a party, right? They've had dinner, a few glasses of wine and now they're with their mates in a theatre, listening to a replication of their favourite singer's tracks. They've also done exactly as they were sold to – I mean, told to, which was to party.

By continuing to court pop musician's back catalogues and further blur the lines (in the audience's minds by way of marketing) between concert, tribute and a theatrical presentation, then we may need to put up and shut up on this one. Unless we wish to secretly undo some of what we've created?

COLLABORATIONS

Over your career you will find some people with whom you artistically click.

Hold them tight and resolve to work together forever (on and off).

VISION

…is a tricky thing. It can feel a bit clumsy if you try too early to describe your production's vision, but you may need to have one quite early on in order to be able to sell it.

The first time you need to quantify your vision will more than likely be when filling in an application form for a festival, for some funding or on a venue's booking form – which can often happen whilst you're still making the show. This may feel a little bit premature, but I actually find it quite liberating, as by the time I have finished filling it in, I will have been forced to give my production some much-needed content and structure when it didn't appear to have any.

BRAND 'ME'

The artist's ego is a thing. It's a necessary, delicious little evil that keeps us stepping out onto the stage. We all have one – and it must be preserved and monitored as it can also be our undoing.

Yup – we all know some artist who doesn't possess an internal behaviour monitor. The kind of artist that fills the room with noise, laughter and mostly themselves. They are a great performer and have worked really hard on their craft, but something's not right.

I know someone like this. They have curated their career based on their artistic-ego, on the image of themselves – and this lets off a stink. The brand of *Them* overrides anything worthy of note. It's a shame because if they could just place their personal objectives aside for a moment, they will truly be lifted to the messianic level they so openly and obviously desire.

THE FIRST TIME

There's a moment in greyhound racing where the trap lifts and the dogs run around the tracks like maniacs after a fake hare.

Opening night can sometimes feel like this. That we must all obtain the fake hare at all costs. I believe this needs to be renounced and that we should explore a way of peace, focus and confidence – because after all, the drama must remain on the stage.

Bake this ideology within everything you do.

WRITING CREDITS

Here are some artistic billing sentences that you might find useful if you've helped write a show, but aren't the main writer:

'With contributions by…'
'With additions by…'

If you've directed a show but also devised material, consider jettisoning the term director all together:

'Made by Them and You.'

I've done this before and it saved me from being artistically annexed. I had written text, devised sections, and invested my own money so 'Made by…' felt right.

A LIST OF FORGOTTEN PRODUCTIONS

BUDDY UP

When creating any marketing campaign, consider buddying up with another company or group of actors. There may be some like-minded artists who would jump at the chance to have a banner of theirs on your mailouts and, likewise, you may find it also benefits you. Check out their work first and then consider if their audience might also enjoy your show.

THE MONA LISA

When you have a piece of theatre or a moment in your show that works, for the most part – don't change it.

I was once fortunate enough to be paid to extend something I'd made with a long-term collaborator. This was a lovely opportunity to revisit our work, but we did seriously think about it first as we had created what we deemed to be a perfect sixty-minute experience and were unsure if we actually wanted to unpack it all again and stick a new face on it.

Thankfully we dodged this bullet by remembering the spirit of our original rehearsals. We added some nuances, inserted a few sections, and jumped deeper into the universe we'd already made, whilst preserving what we had established. By colouring her in a bit and adding some hills in the background, we lovingly enhanced our *Mona Lisa*.

WHAT DID IT ALL MEAN?

Once you have created your production and it's nearing the end of its run, ask yourself: 'What has it communicated?'

Did your choice of font chime with the production? Did the props earn their place in the world of the play? Was your marketing campaign targeted in the right way?

Basically, what did you produce and did it serve the showing?

ART MEETS BUSINESS

The business side of my job is always secondary because the creative side leads and must be protected from the business. In fact, I'd be so bold as to say that I think business should become more creative. Sounds fun, eh? So with this in mind, what would you do if you could infect the formal part of your production with more creativity? Think about your poster, webpage, fan-base, marketing, imagery and finances for a minute – what would happen if you put your business through the question 'Why now?'

ART MEETS MANAGEMENT

You will at some point meet someone who wants to produce your show. This is super-exciting and very, very validating. When you have decided that this producer is for you (after detailed investigation of their intentions and body of work), you will have to relinquish some control but – if you've chosen wisely – it will be a fantastic feeling to let this happen (even if a little strange). Like the parent giving over their child to the teacher for the first time, hoping they'll remember to feed and water them, you must be confident that you've done your research and then you must trust that they know their job.

Make sure you communicate your expectations clearly and have read your contract. Remember, you are an independent artist that has got where they are today by your ambitions and drive – you are not about to throw it all away.

ART MEETS PROBLEMS

Like any other business, you will run into some issues. With theatre, however, the smallest obstacle can be particularly stressful and completely fracture the fragility that live art demands.

The dream scenario is that you're touring a few venues and that, for the most part, the infrastructure surrounding you has been robust and reliable. Your tickets have sold well and when you rock up to the theatre, your posters are clearly displayed. The venue manager shows you to your dressing room, you get given the WiFi password and your tech time. When you begin, the stage manager has read the script and already plotted your lighting cues, and the front-of-house staff checks in with you regularly. You are very happy and any anxiety has melted away and now all you need to do is your job: perform the show. In short – everything is like it was in your head.

Unfortunately, you may… Wait, I'm not gonna lie – you *will* come across situations where none of the above happens. None of it. You could arrive at your allotted time and no one is at the theatre. The venue is shut and you won't have a contact number. Yes, this happened to me; the venue manager

expected the new, part-time box-office staff member to let us in, but hadn't told them our arrival time. When we finally got in, I asked them the way to the studio space, at which point they said, 'We haven't got a studio.' I showed them the theatre's website and my booking form. Anyway, we all discovered the studio that day, only to learn it was without any power and that we weren't allowed to use the lighting desk until the manager arrived. There were no strip lights either so we all used our phone torches for an hour until the stage manager arrived; at which point they said that we were operating our own lights tonight as no one was booked. I showed them the contract, and you bet that night our lights were operated by a set of gritted teeth who we'll call 'Barry'. I bought Barry a pint after the show; he revealed that the venue management hadn't paid him in nearly a month. What can you do when there's this level of incompetence and your precious, delicately planned show isn't being taken seriously? How do you preserve the art? Getting my deposit back and never going back there was my only option.

WORKSHOPS ON YOUR SHOW

There may come a moment in the life of your show or company where you will be asked to teach or find a way to deliver an educational workshop based on your piece. This is great news. Can you teach? If you haven't, never, ever underestimate the skills required. Teaching is a particular craft and often dismissed as just the sharing of information. A bit like the actor who thinks acting is just learning lines, the person who thinks they can teach by spouting some facts is doomed.

A few tips…

Plan the session. If it's two hours, plan for two-and-a-half. Check the delegate numbers, experience, age and then write the workshop to fit those requirements. Prepare for odd numbers and have adaptive exercises ready. Is there a maximum cap on attendance you wish to impose? What's the space like? Whatever happens, take a small portable speaker as some venues will claim to have equipment but it might be broken, locked away or not compatible with your devices. Plan the session with breaks. Are there other teachers in the workshop? Research the establishment you're in. Are you team teaching? If so, divvy up the activities.

Next, break down which part of the show you're going to focus on and mix up the style of interrogation by using music, script and movement. If you feel bold enough, it's quite nice for some people to present their findings at the end. Like a play, design and lightly script your session and, if you're really clever, your whole class (including the warm-up) will be thematically linked to your work.

TICKET PRICES

Currently, tickets for shows in independent spaces seem to be creeping up to £15 and I think the public is on board with this.

What do you think? How much would you pay to see your show, and how much do you want to earn each night?

HOW MANY COMPS?

In a week's run I would comp the following:

Writer: 4

Performers: 2 to 4 each

Press: I remain flexible but stringent on who reviews; they have to have a profile or at least a decent portfolio of thoughtful reviews that are focused on theatremaking and not themselves.

Caveat: I'm going to suggest to you now (and see if you can spot it along your travels) that a lot of people who also make theatre expect free tickets. I think this should be managed better. Yes, there's the argument of the poor artist not being able to afford theatre tickets, but maybe their path towards solvency is by way of not giving away too many of their own tickets?

Remember, you're offering a service and deserve to be paid for it.

WHO TO INVITE?

You should know where you will find your audience.

You should know where you won't find your audience.

You must also be prepared to target an audience that you think will like your show.

You should know which reviewers you'd like to see your show.

Inviting an agent? Educate yourself on them first. If you're looking for representation, don't just take any old hack – do your research, then cherry-pick a few. Agents must provide you with work so check they actually have the contacts.

Theatremakers must be entrepreneurs, so take a few risks with some educated choices.

SELF-CARE

There is an overhanging mindset from the past that the artist, in pursuit of being counter-culture, must go down the darker roads of self-harm. That their work will only be truly nourished and appreciated on a much deeper level if they're drunk or high. This myth was made up by someone drunk or high.

As an athlete of the theatre, it would be nothing short of self-sabotage if you got obliterated before a show. You should be firing on all cylinders, not hitting yourself in the shins before the race.

Sure, kick back on occasion, but for the most part, preserve your consciousness because you cannot see the world and hear its cries if you are in a coma.

THE WRITER

It's been said that the writer is the most creative role in the theatre. I think if you look at it from the point of view that the writer is the genesis of pre-written, text-based work, it's true. That, without Shakespeare, the Globe wouldn't exist.

Now, this idea could be slipping away, as the fluid theatremaker occupies some of the writer's space. But, as we have discussed before, the ability to write can be easily underestimated. Don't be that person. Dive into this skill set with your eyes and ears open, soaking everything up.

THE PERFORMERS

Anxiety is a key factor for performers and, if you're leading on a production, you are, in part, responsible for managing it. It's your job to ease any concerns where possible, as not only do you want people to feel happy and free, you also need them to open their soul every night, and no actor will trust you with their heart if you don't know nor understand how to facilitate some steps towards this.

If there is an issue, listen to their concerns and solve what you can. If there are problems that you don't feel equipped to deal with, remain available and in touch with the situation as you deem to be appropriate.

YOU

There will be many moments where everything falls away. Your production is over and the figures are in. This is the moment you must allow your artistic spirit to evolve and maybe even to heal.

Journalling about it might help: remembering the little dramas that used to be so big, reflecting on any investment anxieties you had before, and asking were they justified? Also, ask: 'What did I learn?' Think of it as an appraisal given by you.

BUDGETS

Keep an eye on them.

INVEST

Four years ago I was at a real mental sticking point. My bloody-mindedness, still resolutely screaming 'I'm going to do the thing that I love forever no matter how tough it gets', took me to my financial edge.

I was trying to create more time for my theatremaking and ditch the teaching gigs I didn't enjoy any more – which was a very thin line to tread, never mind making it even thinner. During this transition I had insomnia and so I thought I needed to hear from an expert on debt and see if it helped to ease things up. I searched 'debt' on YouTube and found a remarkable documentary that asked the viewer to differentiate between your debts and your investments.

This. Was. Life. Changing.

Anyway, my 'debts' are now my 'investments'. I don't have big holidays or own property, but I have invested in a decent computer so I can edit my films and some audio equipment for rehearsals. I also invested in an advert on a prolific theatre website which resulted in more ticket sales and I got some free stuff with it. I am a professional business, and I must invest in its future.

FUTURISTIC THEATRE

Theatre is a very old art and, at the beginning of the twenty-first century, I believe we've still not tapped into its relationship with the internet.

In 2019 a very successful Twitter account (of a fake celebrity) became a live Edinburgh show. It wasn't great, but I thought that it signalled something – that the pipeline of the internet into the theatre could be a thing. The trick is to theatricalise the new whilst still serving the old, immovable gods.

RECOMMEND EACH OTHER

Throughout your career, you will meet artists you click with. Keep this network. They are your tribe.

If you can recommend someone for a job, suggest three or four names from your tribe – and you bet that gift will come back to you one day. In 2015 I got three jobs on the back of one I did in 2014, and all of them were by recommendation of an actor I'd worked with.

EVERYONE MUST GET INVOLVED

Selling tickets is everyone's responsibility. If you are working in a handsomely funded venue then maybe there is a department responsible for ticket sales, but until that day, you must all do your bit.

In fact, always do your bit.

ONWARDS

Many barriers will be thrown in your way over your career. Spot them, then skip around them – whilst whistling.

WORLD DOMINATION?

Let's say you have a company with three or four members in it, and you've come together with the idea that you want to make theatre. Great. Now that's out of the way – what else do you all want from this? World domination? Lead roles? Directing experience? Money? Unless these questions are asked and (albeit temporarily) answered, you'll be sat around a lot waiting for someone to take control, and that's not really the way your dream should be born, is it? A common purpose with a dividing up of the roles is a much more desirable first step.

How to solve this problem? Production meetings. If we are a trade that prides itself on speaking the truth and finding the meaning in things, then this is a moment when we should apply it to ourselves.

IT'S A THING

Over your theatremaking career you will follow your nose from one project to the next based on what interests you. There may be a running theme or a disparate library of interesting topics on your shelf.

Like paintings in a gallery to be admired, marvel at them occasionally – reminding yourself that they were once ideas that you made into things and that they could be made public once again. Be proud, then go ahead and make some more things.

DOCUMENT IT

Invest in documenting your show. Where possible, make sure it's a high-quality video with photos to boot, because remember: you're a professional theatremaker.

PRODUCTION SHOTS

Always invest in a decent photographer that has live-photography experience. Check out their portfolio and, when you're happy, talk to them, laying out your expectations. Maybe find some examples from other productions which you like?

Your photographer is a guest star in your professional ecosystem and is super-important, so make sure they fit and are not an added stress.

WHEN SHOWS DON'T SELL

I want to sell a ticket. It is always my priority. If my show does not sell I must reflect and figure out why. I must dig deep and ask myself if I have focused on the right audience? It could be that the world is not interested in this show right now. Although I love it, the box office does not. For now.

PART 3
MAKING
A COMPANY

I often work with the same people, but we've never spoken about having a company together. We gather to create work and then handle our finances separately. But, for the time we are creating a show, we are most certainly a company of artists.

It seems to be quite a default setting, doesn't it? To graduate or meet someone you creatively click with and then assemble a company immediately. Personally, whenever I have had one (for the briefest of times), they've been – for the most part – a pain in my arse, all because of the added administrative demands.

If I were ever to do it again I'd only go ahead with the correct advice and financial support to help me with the infuriating admin and bureaucracy.

More inside…

START A REVOLUTION

If you don't become a company, what are you? A collective? A movement? A revolution? Find a new concept.

AVOID COPYING INNOVATORS

There have been quite a few groundbreaking companies that have emerged over the last twenty years. Some are movement-based, some absurdist – others community-focused. Of course, you should research them – but don't simply copy them; they are them and you are you. Yes, some may have interesting techniques that are fun to study on occasion in a workshop, but after letting it all soak in, walk away, primed to find your own techniques.

CHANGE PARTNERS

Why work with the same set of people
again and again?

WORDSMITHS

Wordsmiths are verbally dexterous wonders, the superheroes of words. They don't learn words, they are words. They don't study how to internalise words as they are already inside them. Wordsmiths are more than a performer, more than a performance. They're an unstoppable force, a plot with a heartbeat, a page-turner in a costume – and your company must be filled with these communication junkies.

Have a look at Denise Gough, Viola Davis, Johnny Flynn and the late Chadwick Boseman. Learn why Judi Dench and Julie Walters are so valued, and understand the deciding factors as to why Ayushmann Khurrana, Lucy Liu, Brad Dourif and Giovanni Ribisi do it for people. Create a cult of wordsmiths.

SLOW DOWN?

When starting a company you'll forecast this, talk about that, and definitely imagine large projects. There'll be about four or five ideas for a name – maybe even a logo. This is all super-fun and very useful for an hour or two.

After this has all been laid out and you've done a few test sessions to check you have creative chemistry, slow down a bit – you may end up applying for funding or entering into a festival before you even have a clue who you really are and what you want to make.

Think about it: what comes first? The show or the company? An application and then the show? Personally I prefer to have my concept partially manifest and then sniff out where its home may be.

THE 40+ MARKET

A quick flare in the sky…

For the most part, people over the age of forty tend to have a bit more money to spend on leisure activities. If they don't like traditional plays or musicals, or are seeking something a bit more radical, where do they go? I believe we may be missing a trick.

PAY TRAVEL

If someone is a guest star in your collective then please at least offer to pay some of their travel within their fee. I have no idea how you will pay for stuff (ticket sales presumably), but there's something wonderful in adding a contribution to an actor's travel.

About ten years ago there was a popular concept born amongst theatremakers to 'scratch' new material. Unfortunately for the most part, they became evenings synonymous with some very shaky ideas – believe me, I did the legwork. Performers, desperate to utilise the opportunity to be in front of a crowd, flooded the stages with random content, and the venues, more than happy with their full houses, jumped at the chance. Great.

But the audience were charged for this experiment, which after a while made my fur prickle because I felt like I was paying to witness a learning process; that I was serving the performer. And yes I know, I have free choice and didn't have to go – but I want to dig down for a moment into this 'safe space for experimentation' idea in our trade.

I don't want to pay to see a trapeze artist practise; I want to see them perform. I want my taxi driver to have passed their test and my doctor to know how to use a scalpel. Why?

Because I desire skill and dedication from professionals and theatre – professional theatre – must be mindful of how many public pay-per-view experimentations they allow, as the trade could be diminished as a result, and the artist may inadvertently jettison any responsibility and instinct they have to their one job.

So who's being cheated here? Well, arguably, both the audience and the performer are – but I'd add that by way of using a professional setting for scratching, we may present our trade as a space for fledglings and not for solid, skills-based entertainment. To charge an audience on a professional stage to witness scholarship is potentially arrogant and it will be to the detriment of live theatre and our standing if we go too far down that road.

By all means share, but don't charge. If you do charge, it's always, in the audience's mind, a real, actual show – and it should be in ours.

Scary stuff, eh?

PREVIEWS

If you have a preview period, the live-show team (performers, crew and maybe the director to a point) remain focused on bringing all of their dramaturgical wrangling and final decisions to the stage. And, in an ideal world, the producing faculty now moves sideways into the more public-facing side of their role by managing the concept of the preview. This could be handling comps, bar tabs, last-minute issues or simply just being present.

This is a necessary split, but if you've divided up the roles correctly, rest in the knowledge that everyone is still doing their bit to get the show on.

THEATRE WILL REMAIN

We all know that live performance is one of the oldest art forms in the world, so when your company is forming, do some really deep research on the ones that have survived, or on the companies that have broken new ground. More often than not they will have had a deep discussion about the world going on within their infrastructure and will have mixed up the game.

Remember when I said that you don't want to be forgotten? This goes for your company too. Look around; who's creating a company right now and who is not playing by the rules? There's your target to evolve from.

FORMALISE YOUR COMPANY

Did you ever get taught how to set up a theatre company?
Me neither.

Don't panic. The procedure of setting up a theatre company
is the same as setting up any company. Do an internet
search on how to formalise your venture in the country you
live in, and then find the correct path towards registering it
as a business.

WHAT ARE YOUR POLITICS?

There will always be a sense of politics underlying what I
make. Hopefully.

The word 'politics' is usually associated with politicians,
but you can reframe it to your opinions on something.
Ask: 'What are my politics inside the show I'm making or
the company I'm forming?'

ARTS ADMIN

Some companies and institutions have got arts-admin bloat. The more and more investment they've received, the more administration and micro-systems have been created around it, giving the illusion of super-intelligence. Don't be intimidated. They don't hold the secrets to making amazing theatre any more than you or I do.

Remember: art runs your show, and the smaller you are, the more nimble you may be.

FUNDING LOSS

I wrote this thought before the Covid situation temporarily wiped out all live art – however, even before it did, I was wondering if companies that have been handsomely funded for over a decade would survive if their funding ever stopped. Would this be acceptable? How would it be viewed? Could the collapse of a large, prolific venue be justified when the money has been plentiful? Does charitable status really work for theatre?

I am a theatremaker who's never applied nor received any external money, so I happily stand on the outside asking this question.

NEW YORK

I had a great time in NYC remounting an old show. I was in the privileged position of being paid for the gig, so I had little in the way of anxiety during my time there. The show was already a hit with five years of reviews, so we knew it would sell, and in some ways it was such a luxury to do it all again off-Broadway.

What did I learn? Unions are strong in America; there is nothing like our indie theatremakers sector over there; there's no theatre-above-a-pub concept; and everything seems to be quite regulated. We also had a subscription audience which is a very strange beast indeed – it meant we had people rocking up not quite knowing what they were about to see.

CANADA

Again, the same show and model as in New York. A very prolific theatre producer housed us in Toronto and it was all rather wonderful; plus I got another job out of it. I found Canadian theatre to be the exact twin of New York with a peppering of London's spirit. It's still not as free as the arts scene in the UK, given its union rules, but there's a deep love of the arts that seems less commercial, unlike in the US where there appears to be a drive always to find and sell the Next Big Thing.

EDINBURGH

Think of this thought as a precursor to your deeper investigation of the Edinburgh Fringe. There are a million blogs, books and documentaries out there – the most truthful ones being by the artists who've lived it. I am in no way an expert, but I have taken work there a few times; here's what I've learned…

If you take your own show, *really* do your research on which venue will work for you. When you know which one you are in, ask other performers who've performed there about their experiences and to share any tips. See if you can learn the footfall paths around your area that could contain potential ticket-buyers and consider flyering there first. Find out what are the most popular shows that year and ask why?

Your lighting options are very limited in most venues, so consider any blackouts, your get-in, set-up and tech time. If you're using your own money, accept that it's an investment and that you are probably aren't going to get it back in cold, hard cash, but that it will pay you back by way of nourishing your experience and portfolio.

Remember, stay small and nimble. Create your own version of the festival and don't compete with others, or else you may end up punching above your weight. Bigger really isn't always better.

See as much as you can, and be mindful to step out and go to the other festivals – the Television and Book Festivals being my favourites. They are a wonderful side-step and will nourish you in your own work. Oh, and don't drink too much.

VAULT FESTIVAL

VAULT is London's winter festival under Waterloo Station, thought the pandemic regrettably forced the cancellation of two festivals running. It's a vibrant hub for theatremakers to show new work, with some occasional producers scouting for shows.

Practical advice: try and be a self-contained production that slots into VAULT so that you are low maintenance for the team – but do still engage with the festival itself. Have your show copy and hero image – your main, font-free poster image – ready ASAP as you'll need to slot it into VAULT's poster format once you've been accepted.

It's the same twenty-to-twenty-five-minute get-in and get-out as Edinburgh and with a limited backstage and storage space.

TRAILERS

Trailers have more importance in the theatre now, which is weird, because they're films. Anyway, my current view is, unless I have decent footage and sound of my show, I will create something individual – a piece in itself that provokes interest. It'll still be related to the show's marketing and discussion, but with no actors' faces.

In my trailer for *Warped* by Martin Malcolm, I knew I needed to honour the content of the play which discussed idolisation and masculinity in a plot involving two young men on a quest to become notorious British gangsters. In my mind, I kept seeing suited-and-booted men walking down the street. I found some footage of smartly suited men walking, invested £15 in it, got some free music from an indie-site – and began to craft my trailer. The title, *Warped*, was very useful to me in this process, as it epitomised the play's discussion: two strange boys with a bizarre view of the world… so I played the footage backward in the trailer. It ending up looking… warped.

MINUTES
OF MEETINGS

Whatever happens, always make notes during your company meetings; make sure you know who said what, and who is in charge of anything that needs actioning. After the meeting, somebody also needs to compile all of the notes and send them out to the team.

TWITTER

I have been on Twitter for ten years and I find it useful as
a news aggregator. It shows me what is happening in the
world and how people are discussing it. Yes, at times it
may raise your profile and get you some work, but unless
you can prove that it had a direct impact on you gaining
employment, I think it's mostly a very useful news-streaming
and announcement service.

Like with all social media, I always ask myself: 'How can I
use this to nourish my career and contribute to my trade?'
A useful word: nourish. Not 'further' it. I did get offered a
job once via Twitter, a job which gave rise to another – but
besides that, I just use it to study my trade, share interesting
articles and creative quotes. I also make a conscious effort
to share articles beyond the mainstream, UK-based ones
– everyone will tweet and retweet those – because when I
set up my account I asked: 'What could I bring to the table
that's new'? It turns out: quite a bit; now I'm followed by
some very interesting artists and venues, not for my profile,
but for my discussions on theatre.

When I have an account for a show, again it's the same
approach. What else can I tweet about that's not just based
on 'buy my tickets now'? I also do not set up an account
for every show; they seem to me to be temporary echo
chambers that go silent on the last night, or if the show is
never made.

FACEBOOK

When Facebook first emerged I was very uncomfortable with it. I remember thinking that it seemed like a huge exercise in vanity. I was on it, off it, and now I'm on it again. As it evolved, though, and I contemplated it further, I now feel I have tamed it, and use it for its strengths. I currently have a blank profile that you must have (at the time of writing) to host any other pages. From this, I have my main Russell Lucas page which I use to share or contemplate live art or film. I have about 160 followers and that suits me fine. Does it sell tickets? Maybe. To my friends.

I do have one other for a show I made, and that is very successful; not only do we share news about the next performance, but also content about the themes of that show.

So it seems, if you can tame these sites for your own purposes, and bend a few rules, they're super-useful.

INSTAGRAM

Facebook appears to be for friends and groups, Twitter for news and corporations, and Instagram for the individual/business and their visual value. I have tried Instagram and although I get it, my Twitter and Facebook seem to work quite well for me right now, so taking on something else doesn't seem a useful step. Young adults really love it, though – important to note, eh?

If I was to run an account, I'd focus on the visual aspects of my job. Costumes, props, faces, movement, posters, scenes – anything that grabs the eye.

Okay, now even I'm tempted.

THEATRE CATEGORIES

Musical Theatre has it in the name, as does Physical Theatre, Immersive Theatre, Youth Theatre and Children's Theatre. Hell, we even have Dinner Theatre now.

Why not Mime Theatre? Storytelling Theatre? Voice-Installation Theatre?

What is *your* theatre?

CABARET

Cabaret is performance art gone mainstream. It's circus with songs; it's musical theatre that's eaten itself; it's drunk-drag; it's pantomime in July; it's the entrance to heaven through a burning glitter curtain; it's torture with a feather; it's titillation with a chainsaw; and it's the perfect space for your nan to sing a few Vera Lynn songs.

In short, it's one of the most pliable art-forms for a theatre company to utilise.

SCHOOL TOURS

I toured schools in the nineties. It was the classic model: six of us in a van travelling around the county, playing three schools a day with our forty-five-minute devised play. We had three or four shows ranging from topics as diverse as pregnancy, recycling and bullying – we'd written them ourselves and we toured for at least three years. It was exhausting and at times mind-numbing – but the things I learned were endless…

…Speed, pace, stage management, impro, shape, dramaturgy, collaboration, commissioning, writing, deadlines…

Tempted?

APPLIED THEATRE

I suspect if you dig deep, this term will be born from academia somewhere, but in its simplest form, it's theatre for a specific space or audience. Or is that site-specific theatre? I'm not sure what that title means either as surely all theatre is site-specific?

Anyway, these labels come and go – smile sweetly and just make some theatre for the world you exist in now.

TOURING

A friend of mine once lamented that the UK touring model is broken. On one level, I agree. Unfortunately.

So what does this mean? That you're on your own as you'll more than likely be organising your own tours, travel and accommodation. It's not impossible to work this way, and you may actually be going back to the old vagabond ways I lamented the loss of before, but I guarantee you're still needed, required even, to keep the theatre scene vibrant and eclectic – and you need to keep the country connected by way of new stories.

Is this you? Are you the person to rethink and recalibrate the touring model?

STRANGE VENUES

There are venues run by people who probably shouldn't be running theatres. There, I said it. Yes, I know, everyone can work in the theatre, but you've still got to know how to do the job. Now, I'm not going to name theses places as they'll reveal themselves to you along the way, but how do you manage them? I think the best advice I can offer you is: don't try to. You are but a visitor passing through that can't fix any inconsistencies within their infrastructure, so learn to mentally walk away from any issues.

The only thing you must protect is your show and the audience's experience. Always, *always* aim to have an anxiety-free day; so prepare as much as possible. If something fails, dodge the panic and be prepared to sacrifice things to ensure that your delivery goes smoothly. Don't absorb any of the drama created by incompetence. Remember you're out of there in six hours and you can make a note to never come back.

TALK TO OTHERS

Theatremaking can be a solitary life. No one cares about your project as much as you, right? So how can we survive the process without having feelings of isolation and crippling tremors in our self-confidence? I'm not sure we can, is the brutal answer, but I feel that (in the long term) these are healthy responses, as they are based on a genuine reaction to your surroundings. The trick is learning how to spot them and then asking for some help.

We all live in our little creative bubbles, our version of the trade, and we can sometimes forget there's a lot of solidarity around – you just have to seek it out. A trick I do on occasion is to try and identify what my anxiety is focusing on, and then solve it immediately, in however small a way.

Anxiety is fear of the unknown, so all you have to do is dig down on the top layer of your fear. Let's say that you are worried about ticket sales. You're up at 3 a.m. and have mild insomnia. After identifying that sales are your issue, go to the venue's website and find a few shows that have been on at the same venue as yours. Find their email and in the morning, message them asking them how it went, and could they offer up any ticket-selling tips? You may be surprised how many people respond and you will have done something positive towards relieving your tension.

Send up a distress signal and someone will see it.

ACCOUNTS

Do them.
Find an accounting method that works for you.
Keep track of every expense.
Keep your receipts.
Be strict with tax deadlines.
Stay on top of invoices and statements.
Get advice from other artists.

MARKETING MEETINGS

This is where the creative side must meet the business again. If I'm honest, unless marketing concedes that it is in service to the creatives and sometimes needs to get out of the way, it can undo the work very easily.

I'm not going to go into too much depth here because if you want to learn about theatre marketing all you have to do is keep your eyes open, remain curious as to what's working and, more importantly, spot what needs updating. Remember everything serves the discussion, the plot and the world you have created.

WALK AROUND THE ROOM

A quick thought about originality. If you want your company/ensemble/movement to be an original beast, there are other minute ways for you to mix things up other than what type of theatre you create, and checking in with any habits you may have picked up over the years is one of them.

One of the age-old sentences actors hear before they begin a session is 'Walk around the room'. Once this instruction has been uttered, performers, dutifully, walk around the room. Why? Because they've spent their whole career up to this point doing that, so what's one more round? This is a regular theatre environment and regular theatre company, right?

Wrong. Freak them out. Mix it up. Shift it to 'explore the space' or walk in a spiral, anything but 'walk around the room'. It's the same with sitting in circles; change it to a square or sit on your hands. Try a warm-up without speaking and feel the energy shift. Anything. Go wild. This may seem like a ridiculous thought, but trust me; thinking differently is the key to creating differently and everything must be up for change.

LEAP

It's well documented that resistance is usually rooted in fear of the unknown, and making a company and creating live art at the same time, without being able to forecast the future, is going to be a test of your fortitude. It's true to say that fear raises its ugly head often, but I've learned to hot-wire my brain back to resilience – and to trust myself. So I reckon it's the resistance stage you must watch out for. That's where experimentation dies and conflicts arise. But how do you spot this and learn to ride it out? To make sure it doesn't sabotage discovery?

Leap.

When you are making up excuses for not doing something, do it anyway. Obviously don't hurt anyone or put yourself in any danger – but just go for it. The unknown may be what you fear, but you're a resilient artist, or you will be, the more and more you leap.

ACTION
AND PLOT

Action is an objective (a physical or verbal doing) on the way to accomplish a purpose. The plot is the unfolding of action to reach a conclusion.

PAUSES

'Pause': another archaic term that needs to be retired from the theatre's dictionary.

A 'pause' written in a script in today's world signifies a writer still trying to control the actor. If you write a pause in your play, then you'll get one alright as everyone grinds to a halt every night because you were once sitting at your desk and thought, 'Hmm, they should pause here.'

There's really no need for these dead moments any more. If you feel super-passionate about a particular moment, make a note for later on. Once you've watched the actor live your words, see if that pause survives; or if you even remember it. They should know what they are doing and if you feel they don't, walk away and find a new team. If you're deft enough, they'll read the text with your pause because your prose forces them to do it.

Pause on this thought.

AN ACTOR LEAVES

In your travels you will come across situations where someone will, for whatever reason, drop out of your production/company. I've had a few over the past two decades – mostly related to personal issues. There have also been some situations that were rooted in a lack of confidence in rehearsals.

If this happens to you: first, remain open and available to the actor who has left the show; and second, preserve the production.

DESIRES

I mean, come on; what do you want from your company? Global domination? A major theatre brand? A venue? Three venues? Three hundred venues? To break the mould? To remain in a mould? Community work? A school's programme? To tour? Equipment? Costumes? Logo? Website? To be worshipped? An educational arm? To restart the rep model of theatre? Five stars every time? To host a festival? Merch? Mailing list? To be known as the greatest theatre company ever? To be effective? To take down the government? To rebuild a government? To perform in the streets? To go into film? To be a charity? To earn a wage? A pension? To get time off? To be sustainable? To be eco-friendly?

BUSINESS MEETINGS

...are necessary.

DICTATORSHIP

In the theatremaking process, there's always someone or something in charge, an entity making the final decisions that steer the ship into the harbour. Of course, companies will claim to create by way of ensemble, but I bet – if you dig deep – that such companies will have a very strong didactic strategy somewhere that has been decided by predetermined power structures; that they are already following a direction, however cleverly it's been hidden and infused into the company technique.

GAMES

Whoever introduced games into the theatremaking canon was most definitely an academic or a scholar of improvisation. Or a director killing time.

Whenever I deliver a workshop, I find myself delivering these rather dull games. Why? The actors appear to enjoy them whilst everyone else looks over their scripts from the sidelines thinking, 'Aww, bless…'

Personally I hate delivering them. I'm not a games master, nor a children's entertainer. I understand the point of them in that it gets the energy up and keeps us playful, but a run around the block can do that. Artistic-enhancing activities are now my preferred route.

Should we abandon the games? Yes. Up for it?

MIND GAMES

If they occur, remain focused on the work.

ART

Your successful company must be anchored in art – the art-focused company that raises itself above the norm and pushes the genre forwards is one that will survive. But then what do I mean by art? What is art in a live-art context?

Art seems to be the assembling and application of ideas put together to present to an audience in a particular order. Is that art? Yes, absolutely it is. You are an artist. I crown you now.

But do avoid just putting something on stage for the sake of it. If you're blocking a play, that's not art; it's choreography. If you're writing 'pause' in your script, it's the opposite of creativity, isn't it? Build up your expectations of the art form and reshape the land with your version of theatre.

HONESTY

When you have an issue in the company, either with someone else or about something that is happening within the group, it is better to be honest ASAP. Talk about how you are currently feeling rather than wait for things to suddenly burst out of you.

If you do need to talk to anyone or indeed the whole company, send them all an email and ask for a quick chat after rehearsals or even before and say you'd like to talk about X, Y or Z. By doing this you give it some air, rather then springing something on them the next day. Come to the meeting with your issue and frame it by removing any blame. Offer up some solutions and finish by asking everyone their thoughts. After the meeting, thank them in an email stating what was discussed.

Adult discussion works for a reason.

A WEEK TO GO

There's always a moment when we seem to be treading water in the theatremaking process. It's usually about a week before the show opens: all of the fun stuff is completed and you are now in the slalom towards the edge. It's the most precarious time where everyone feels vulnerable, because not only have the stakes suddenly been raised, but you may be reaching a state of exhaustion and fear.

If you are in that space – and if you can – take some time off; just a few hours away from anything to do with theatre to get some perspective can really do wonders. Call an old relative, or watch the rush hour coming home to appreciate what you have done with your life, find a pub by a river – whatever; just do something different. You'll arrive back at rehearsals slightly altered and primed.

PRESSURE

I would say, having worked in most areas of the theatre, that when the show goes up, it is the actor that is under the most pressure – without a doubt.

Hurts, doesn't it? To hear that. It feels unusual.

That's not to say that all of the other jobs aren't pressurised, because of course they are. Through the ever-turning merry-go-round of theatre production, there are times when each role bends under the structure of putting on a show. In rehearsals it's the director, in the tech it's the stage manager and the crew, and on press night it's the producer. But during all these periods, in the centre of it all, is the performer – the conduit and translator of all these micro-pressures.

Of course, we will all chime in and say our roles are always stressful, and the actor will happily bow to you, but – as someone who has directed, produced, performed and stage managed – no one, when the curtain rises, has the weight of responsibility like the actor.

They do love it, though.

ATMOSPHERE

Think of your favourite brand or your favourite shop for a minute. What is it about them that you like? For me, it's the shop COS and the magazine *Monocle*. Both are very contemporary brands with a strong emphasis on design. COS has beautiful clothes and vibrant ideas about how they should be administered to the world. When I walk in I can feel the natural fibres and see the simplistic design of their clothes. With *Monocle*, it's the mature way they report the news of the world. It's connected to community and sustainability and has a very individual voice.

This marketing approach can also be applied to your theatre company. You too can aim for an approach that's unique, that bends the concept of a theatre business. You too can make your customer feel they are being cared for by your product. Theatre is life, styled.

BRAND

I may undo some of my last thoughts with this one, but bear
with me and we'll probably find a middle ground.

It's worth noting that these days the brand of a theatre or
a company can become its driving force over everything. I
don't think it's on purpose, I just think that some institutions
– having to appease their funding body – can be forced into
a 'brand equals power' mindset.

Now, if you look carefully, you'll note that a theatre that is
brand-focused may sometimes be less likely to be theatre-
focused. That somewhere, inside their building is a theatre,
but somehow they've ended up being at the mercy of their
brand imagery, the cult of themselves and, therefore, they
lose sight of their only job – to create life-changing theatre.
So it seems having a strong brand can mean nothing more
than possessing a strong brand.

HIERARCHY

The theatre trade has internalised a rather warped hierarchy – mostly caused by money. If someone has a lot of cash they will be called an industry leader and claim to speak for 'the industry' – which, of course, is a load of codswallop. They just have the clout and the platform to do and say what they please, giving the appearance that they are the invincible experts that live in Theatre Utopia. Again – blah. The 'Top Theatre Producers' list guarantees to fill a newspaper column, not a theatre.

RESEARCH

I love research. I never thought this would happen, having mostly hated academia, but with the rise of online content and alternative news sites, my interest has been very much piqued.

First, I will find some stimuli that are 'about' my topic, but I can't wait to get to the point when I am looking for things that are related to my discussion. The content search is usually online and that will in turn flag up films, music, images and articles. Books are my favourite medium as I get to attack them with my highlighter when I find a little piece of information I want to remember for later on. Galleries can be super-useful too: maybe there's an exhibition somewhere that is related to your discussion?

Anyway, to bring this all back to your company: divvy up the research and then find a time you all come together and share your findings. And – if you really want to shake it up – swap research with each other and have everyone present something back based on someone else's findings by way of a dance or poem – anything to start theatricalising your idea. You never know, one of these presentations may end up being in your show.

GUEST STARS

…are people who are in your company for a temporary time.

Hopefully you have chosen the right artist and that they are ready to work productively and creatively. Of course, you will need to bend on occasion to absorb the way they work and vice versa, but if you remain consistent, concise and transparent, it will be a wonderful shot in the arm to have a new voice in the room that could usher in new opportunities.

A MODERN-DAY SANCTUARY

I feel that theatres must fight hard for their place at the table; for their position within the town they are situated. It's a real trick, isn't it? To lure and entice people into a theatre. Why? Because of our public-image issues. On the one hand we are open to all, and on the other we are – sometimes – over a hundred pounds a ticket. We try to use the 'theatre is at the heart of the community' schtick, but I think community should be at the heart of the theatre. It's not, though. Money and sales are at the heart of theatre and we don't always offer what the public wants – we, more often than not, offer what we think they want or more of what they've had before.

By retreating to the theatre's past, we will inadvertently erode our relevance by way of our own fear. Fear of losing an imagined place at the table, when really what we need to do is usher in some fresh ideas. It's the only way theatre will survive if it is to be a sanctuary for the now and not a museum for yesteryear.

If we keep running towards our old tropes we will remain anchored – no, shackled – to our variety-hall past, inadvertently fast-tracking ourselves to a pub or bingo-hall destination.

YOUR QUEST

Quests are for warriors with a purpose.

GENRES: BEND THEM

Genres. Bend them.

LOOKING
SIDEWAYS

Whenever I look around too much at what others are doing, I find that I'm actually in a vulnerable state and it usually means that I'm comparing myself to them, which is not healthy.

This tendency to fastidiously watch other people's careers has slowly ebbed away over the years as I've grown to care less about what they are doing and have learned to remain focused on my own expected outcomes.

PEOPLE SHOW

I want you to check this company out immediately. They are one of the oldest theatre companies in the UK and are still going some fifty years later.

'We are always shifting shape, actively defying definition...'
People Show

177
SOCIAL-MEDIA ADDICTION

Avoid sharing and engaging with your phone straight after your show. Rest up, pack everything away, go for pizza – whatever. Just slow it all down and listen: your collaborators and the audience are super-important right now, and you don't want to lose an ounce of that information.

Why not schedule a time the next day to engage with your online admin, social media included? It may also be really useful to wait as your media platform's algorithms could be more vibrant in the morning.

178
ACADEMIA TO THE BACK

Theatremaking is an art and that's the end of this sentence.

Of course, academic thought is sometimes very useful in the study of the arts for its historical context and as a tool to analyse meaning, but it all has to – *has to* – fall away at some point. Writing this book is an academic activity, but hopefully I'm bending the theatre 'how to' book genre slightly by offering up some clear and concise, non-academic thoughts for you to digest.

EAT AND DRINK

You're an athlete of the theatre. Run towards feeling good.

OXBRIDGE

The stakes are the same no matter where you come from.

PART 4

MAKING
A TRADE

By the end of your career (remember you're sticking around to see what will happen), you will have created your version of the live-art trade.

That's probably the only thing we share with each other, by the way: our trade. Of course, there's a skill set and shedloads of passion, but the intellectual add-ons of 'industry', 'family' and 'team' appear to be flimsy concepts to help us find the feels on social media or to give the appearance of marching under a banner of a venue or company, but they're not based in any on-the-ground reality. We're all alone on this quest of ours and only we care about our own career.

By the end, your industrious nature will have made you into a leader in a career that you have crafted – no one else. Contracts will come and go, and it will be your diligence that will have made you an expert – not by way of association with a venue or a school, but by you, on your own, ducking and diving inside the business of creating, and then presenting, a live act.

SHOWBIZ

Theatre and show business are one and the same, but I find there's a useful intellectual slicing here, that I occasionally utilise, that saves me from resenting certain elements of the trade – and that area I call '*showbiz*'.

Now, before I go on, I have to admit that part of what I am about to say is more than likely related to my snobbery – my utter dislike of theatre that's shot so far up its own glitter cannon that everyone's exclaiming it's fabulous when it's not quite doing its job properly. The type of theatre where the posters tell me it's a hit, blinding me with their stars on every street corner, and yet when I go and see it, I cannot help but raise an eyebrow and judge this sequinned echo chamber. Or is it the marketing I'm judging? Or the public falling for it again? Or the people involved? Maybe there is no blame here and I have to accept that there's a demand?

If theatre is to survive, and be taken more seriously, showbiz must dial it down a tad – it's becoming white noise, rendering us as a disposable and frivolous pastime. Whilst I know that theatre is escapism, I put it to you that the dial has moved a little too far one way and needs rebalancing.

Showbiz: you've shown us all your bits, jumped the shark, nuked the fridge, and yes, I know, we are BFF – but we have to get better at administering showbiz to a contemporary audience, and to do this we're going to need to turn away from some of our old quick-fix gods.

No matter the genre, let us rebalance this constant celebration of mediocrity, and seek out entertainment with a contemporary relevance, as that's when 'we' are at our best.

CRITICS

For the most part, the experience inside a theatre is a subjective one and that is most evident when you read a rave review of a show on one website and a scathing critique of the same show on another. With this in mind, there's also very little reason to fear the critic these days. Yes, we all want to read nice words about our artistic endeavours and receive five-star ratings in the press, but it seems to be unproductive to allow the fear of them into your head on press night.

Of course, I know that this fear is related to being criticised by someone who knows what they are talking about (hopefully) but, if you've done your homework, the rest will come as it comes – plus, as printed media seems to be ending, audiences are now seeking out what they want.

So get out there, comrades, and do your job to the best of your ability, in service to the *audience*.

SHOULD THEATREMAKERS BE CRITICS?

Most critics are not theatremakers. Of course, they may exist – Kenneth Tynan comes to mind – because someone's decided that they are both, but until I read one of their life-changing critiques *and* then witness one of their successful productions, I think it's safe to say that – for the most part – critics don't make theatre often.

Critics are the outside eye for the public; the filter who, hopefully, asks the important questions like: 'What did they intend to make?' and 'Has it worked?' But remember they're not your theatremaking peers; they're just looking in with a love for live work and a sense for audience tastes.

But – theatremakers who do decide to publicly critique, by crowning themselves a judge of live art, will be assumed to possess a super-authority on the subject – which one day they will need to prove.

UPDATED PRODUCTIONS

There's always a lovely buzz when we witness a new version of an old show. We are reborn and revitalised as it changes and also ups the trade's possibilities. Sometimes theatremakers get it really right; other times, monumentally wrong. So is there a secret formula for making an old show live in a new world?

I've directed a few classic plays and I rarely investigate any past productions as I feel it can muddy my waters a bit. Having said that, it can be difficult to step out of their shadow, as the script you have in your hand may be from that landmark production filled with specific stage directions that you will have to remain blind to. When I directed *Driving Miss Daisy* I knew the expected tropes – so obviously I tried to bend them at every turn whilst drip-feeding expectations. It was fun and felt like the right decision.

So once again, it seems you must give them what they want, and find something new and relevant inside it.

BE KIND TO THE WEST END

I can be very unforgiving when I look at the West End, because sometimes all I see is a jaded and exhausted cyclical commercialism, nesting in a bed of loud sweets and merchandise, that will all end up rotting in a landfill, with queues of audience members desperate to lap it up.

But they're giving the audience what they want. Aren't they?

GATEKEEPERS
ARE NOT ALWAYS
ARTISTIC

It took a while for me to figure this one out.

I went for an interview at a prolific venue once, a theatre I respected and loved. It was for a job to devise and direct a community project. I definitely had the experience to back it up and had done my homework on their idea. During the interview I was met by the head of HR and they sat me down and that was when I noticed they had three questions on a piece of paper… and a three-minute egg timer.

Throughout your career you may meet people who work in the arts who don't have a creative quest, but know how to tick a box. This is a sad truth. The even sadder one is that they may be the one that stops you in your tracks. Temporarily. Accept this, knowing that you don't want them in your world either.

THE INDUSTRY DOESN'T EXIST

The reason I challenge the word 'industry' is that we don't produce anything.

WAIT. What I mean is that we are, at base, just storytellers. That's not an industry, it's a skill set. Of course, we produce published playtexts and T-shirts and CDs and mugs – but that's retail.

We trade in stories.

THE TERM 'REGIONAL THEATRE'

…was invented by a Londoner. Ignore it.

RESTAURANT AND BARS

Many theatres will now have a café filled with sumptuous snacks and beverages, or maybe even a restaurant. They'll often have decent WiFi, quiet areas and space for artists to beaver away on their new work.

This is a great evolution, but is the theatre a slave to it all? Must they now insert an interval to increase their bar sales? Is the restaurant run by the theatre or another company? Do the catering staff know what is on in the auditorium? Is the Artistic Director having to worry more about the price of a packet of crisps than the artistic programme?

So many questions about this model.

CV

Hardly the most creative thing, is it? Thankfully, the older I get I rarely have to send, let alone compile, a CV that is coherent and represents my creativity.

It is getting easier these days, though, to present your profile to a potential employer. PDFs allow you to insert links taking the reader to any online evidence you have; photos can be easily attached. That said, it's still really difficult to state what you are about without it looking like... a CV. And don't get me started on venues trying to shoehorn us all through their expensive online web-portals – yawn.

There is one thing that works for me that I'd like to share, and that's an artistic statement. It seems by prefacing the rather dull listing of my portfolio, a quick paragraph about my schemes and thoughts on live art can raise up the document. Here's mine in 2021:

> *I am a UK-based artist specialising in writing, devising, producing, acting and directing original work. My medium is predominately theatre and I curate online content that studies the journey of other theatremakers. I have directed gallery installation films and delivered workshops in educational settings. Being very much an independent, entrepreneurial artist, my portfolio reflects this as I'm interested in creating new live art, or to present old work in fresh ways.*

Do steal.

SOME PROFESSIONS WILL BE PAUSED

It seems that as the post-Covid world unfolds, some roles within our trade will be paused or even looked back on as jobs from a time of luxury.

I forecast many assistant roles will disappear, as will dramaturgs, as well as positions that used to come under the umbrella of arts admin. Movement directors may struggle too, as will, I suspect, associates.

To offer a lifeline for a second, think what that role is derivative of, or related to, and see if you can change hats to find a way back. Perhaps producing is your next step, or directing? Either way, if you're in it for the long haul – you'll get there.

PAY YOURSELF AFTER EVERYONE ELSE

Let me tell you a story…

A friend of mine would travel to work from another country to work with a theatre company. That company had funding, but sometimes they would not pay my friend their travel – or, if they did, it was never, ever enough. This was astounding to me and I would get very angry at my friend for saying yes to the contract every year – but that's a separate issue.

What was more amazing to me was that the company had money. But when I think about it, this is not uncommon. Whatever you do, always pay everyone else *before* yourself; and while we're at it – pay the actors first because if you have funding and can't pay the actors properly you need to think about your life choice – they are the one thing you will *always* need, and you need *professional* actors.

And actors? You're not blame-free here. If someone has funding and they are not valuing you, address the issue immediately. If they have a successful company that doesn't pay you for weekly rehearsals to support the brand – it's time to turn professional.

A CREATIVE PRODUCER IS ALWAYS DESIRABLE

All producers should be creative producers – creativity is at the heart of producing – so why this new term? Has someone invented an MA on Creative Producing as a partner to their MA on 'just' Producing?

Producers have always been creative. They are the unsung gods of theatre. Who else has a nose for a hit, wisely selects other creatives to work together *and* somehow finds a way to buy everyone a drink?

A producer that is creative is the best kind – in fact: they should be the only kind.

THEATRE AND CHILL?

Will we ever get to the point where we kick back with pizza whilst watching the latest play by James Graham, Arinzé Kene, Lucy Sheen or Satinder Chohan? Will we one day settle into a theatre under our duvets to watch Robert Wilson's twelve-hour 'silent' opera *The Life and Times of Joseph Stalin* under our duvets whilst we live Instagram?

I'm not sure, but let's welcome in the changes whilst remembering theatre is still a live event.

THE UNFUNDED ARE THE MAJORITY

There are many, many artists out there who do not have funding, yet still find a way – but this thought won't chime with the funded, as they seem to presume that you can only work in the arts if you have funding.

You only need to go through the Edinburgh Fringe programme to note that the majority are not funded by anyone but themselves. If this is you, sit comfortably in that space for *you* are the majority. You may not be prolific, but who cares? Make some groundbreaking theatre and the rest will come.

THERE ARE NO INDUSTRY LEADERS

Don't worry about the terms 'leader' or 'leading figure' when they pop up; as I said before, they are meaningless and are only there to fill website and newspaper-column space. It's theatre about theatre.

The other day I read a list of 'Performances of the Decade'... Please.

Other obscene ones: 'The Most Influential' and 'The Richest' – yawn. I browsed their roll-call and could name at least three or four of their tragic artistic flops/early closings they'd all had. It should really be called 'The Top Five Prolific Millionaires Who Will Help Us Sell This Paper and Website' list.

Now, I'm not dancing on their failures here because we will all have them. No, what I'm saying is these lists are meaningless and we must ignore them (or stop compiling them), because they send out a message that there is only one way to make theatre – that their careers are the only path, the only version of success.

I don't want a Famous Rich List, I want twenty-first-century theatre journalism that acknowledges that great theatre can be made in any space by anyone, and to give equal value to the quieter, and equally representative, careers.

Caveat: if theatre publications only speak to the prolific then their time at the table may also be up.

THE THEATRE IS STILL THE ACTORS

X

THE MONSTER
AT THE DOOR

Throughout your career, you will always feel fear. The fear that at any point you may lose everything, that you won't make rent or pay any debts off. Even when you are solvent you will still have this nagging feeling that it's all going to fall apart at some point. This is normal and anyone who takes a weekly paycheque will feel the same at one time or another – believe me.

You, however, have decided to answer your calling and live a life in the arts. This healthy decision – to follow your true vocation in life – is your version of true happiness.

A friend of mine once said, 'This is it, isn't it? We're living the dream, aren't we?' We were at a train station on our way home after rehearsing all day; they were going to do a gig and I was spending the evening planning my creative delivery for a school I was working at – and you know what: they were right.

Every time I'm in the rehearsal room I keep thinking, 'This is it, I'm still here and I know what to do next to make this continue.' How? Because I resolved, decades ago, that *this* is my job.

THE WEST END IS...

LOUD

MUSICALS

GLITTERY AMAZING PLAYS

INSULAR FULL

ART WORK CONSISTENT

DIRTY MAINSTREAM SMALL

URBAN INTENSE CONSERVATIVE

COMPACTED LARGE VICTORIAN

NEPOTISTIC SKILLED

CENTRAL PROFESSIONAL

EDWARDIAN

LUXURIOUS

EXPENSIVE

TRADITIONAL

VENUE OWNERS

…aren't always going to share your vision.

It's an awful truth that you are a visitor to a venue and the proprietor, whilst grateful for the bar and ticket sales you will bring in, just wants you to do your job to the best of your ability.

TRANSFERS

When you look in horror at what you deem to be a questionable piece of theatre being moved into town, know that there's another reason behind it: someone, somewhere, with some money, is taking a punt that they can sell that piece to the public – thus, potentially, recouping the show's original investment.

For some reason we interpret the word 'transfer' as artistic validation, but of course it's not always the case.

THE PROLIFIC

There are (in London) really only about ten agents that actors should try and get with. I'm not gonna name them, but if you have a search they will make themselves apparent. Why these ten? Contacts and decades of fostering relationships.

The next pool of agencies, the other ninety-nine per cent, will have all the same skill sets, but maybe not the clout. This is, of course, rather sad as it means the actors on the top ten agents' books will get a lot of the work.

What can you do about this? Create life-changing theatre and sell it back into the trade – and the agents will come to you.

ONE DAY MORE

Wandering around town in the late nineties I was still caught up in the idea that I should be in one of the West End behemoths; that I would one day be in *Les Mis* or *The Mousetrap*... One day. But when I paid closer attention to its ecosystem, I noticed it was (for the most part) the same players, producers, writers, transfers, stars, reviews and so on and so on... With a few newbies that may have slipped through the net.

The more I thought about it, there really was no place for me there, as I didn't fit – and the closer I got, the more I realised I didn't really want to operate in that type of system. No, if I was going to have a show in town, I would need to go further than my initial ambition and get there under my own steam with agency over my work – which is exactly what happened with *Julie Madly Deeply* in 2013.

AWARDS

You may be offered an award at some point. What do you reckon? Take it? Free bar, maybe. Your call. I guess it hands you some social-media glory?

But what does it mean to be given one? Is it justified? Who's the organisation? Do they have a good record of representation? Who else has won? What was the criteria for the judging panel, and do you agree with it?

ACTORS WHO'VE NEVER BEEN TO THEATRE SCHOOL

Charlie Chaplin
Jennifer Lawrence
Earl Cameron
Idris Elba
Helen Mirren
Eddie Murphy
Ian McKellen
Matthew Jacobs Morgan
Chloë Grace Moretz
Daniel Kaluuya
Nico Santos
Christian Bale
Tom Cruise
Matthew McConaughey
Ben Kingsley
Joaquin Phoenix
Dev Patel
Norman Beaton
Charlize Theron
Adjoa Andoh
Natalie Portman
Marilyn Monroe

DIRECTORS WHO'VE NEVER TRAINED

Most of them.

PRODUCERS WHO'VE NEVER TRAINED

You can see a pattern here, eh?

ONLINE THEATRE

I read somewhere that online theatre is the absence of theatre. I thought this to be a rather wonderful way to describe what I feel when I watch text-based theatre on screen.

When we watch something on screen, we are guided on what to watch by way of the edit. We see what the director wants us to see by way of their choices after the show has been performed. The same is true of online theatre; that we will only ever see what is presented to us on the screen. When in an actual theatre, I can look wherever I like. I can study the show's costumes, I can observe the lighting, get lost in the movement, watch the actors enter and exit and, if I want to, I can even look at the venue's architecture. The online version does not and will never be able to provide this for me.

It is evident, though, that the online version of theatre makes a production much more accessible, but it's not the future of theatre in any way because it's not live. You are not there. They are not in front of you. It's a curiosity – an alternative version – an historical record of a once real, once live act.

But it's not theatre, is it?

UNIONS

Some theatremakers are currently sitting in the gaps
between the pavements.

As we don't perform very often in traditional settings or in
the usual way, we are currently in a no man's land. For now.

You may shunt up against a union at one point and your
rebel heart will have to quell its fire because some people are
very passionate about them. But do your homework as to
why they exist and then make your choice whether or not to
get involved.

MERITOCRACY

'The most common form of meritocratic screening found today is the college degree. Higher education is an imperfect meritocratic screening system for various reasons, such as lack of uniform standards worldwide, lack of scope (not all occupations and processes are included), and lack of access (some talented people never have an opportunity to participate because of the expense, most especially in developing countries). Nonetheless, academic degrees serve some amount of meritocratic screening purposes in the absence of a more refined methodology. Education alone, however, does not constitute a complete system, as meritocracy must automatically confer power and authority, which a degree does not accomplish independently.' Wikipedia, 2021

OTHER TRADES

Having some music composed for your work may not be as expensive as you think. You could find a new composer who might jump at the chance to work on your new project with you.

If you want to stream your show, there may be a start-up company that would like to collaborate with you.

Go shunt up against some other trades.

SET YOUR OWN STANDARDS

What are the expectations of your trade? Write up a list.

Here are a few things I value:

Good, clear and concise communication
Laughter
Freedom
Professionalism
Experimentation
Interrogation
Surprises

WHO ARE THEY?

You'll find yourself saying 'they' a lot: 'They didn't want me', 'They'll probably cast someone famous', and so on. Who are these middle managers that keep you from your audience? Are they rich? Are they influencers? Who is this group you are handing your power to?

EVERYONE'S WRONG

How many 'How to write a play' and 'How to act' books are there on the bookshelves? I expect it to be hundreds if not thousands. Now think of the one everyone cites as the book of acting, the bible of screenwriting. Which ones come to mind? Do you have either on your shelf? If so, do you go back to it every day to check you're following their methods? I doubt it.

If you're like me, I've read the ones I'm supposed to, not really understood them, and then kept my eyes and ears open for the other ones. When I have found the ideas I connect with, I highlight their salient points and keep them on my shelf, ready for the day I need a bit more clarity on my own thoughts. But remember, any advice you get today might be out of date tomorrow.

TEACH?

Teaching opportunities will definitely drop into your lap at some point. I spoke about this before and I asked, 'Can you teach?' Now I ask: 'Do you *want* to teach?'

This is a really important question to ask as there are way too many teachers who work in education that probably shouldn't; and there are many artists who thought, 'I should go into teaching', and find out pretty quickly they should've sat this one out.

When I say teaching, I mean the short-burst workshop kind that you'll either be asked to deliver based on your show or the ones where you'll be hired as an artist to creatively reach a certain group of students.

Do you want to teach? It's nothing like you think it is.

TEACH FULL-TIME?

There have been many artists that have gone into full-time teaching for whatever reason. Bravo, say I. I couldn't do it – my trade is the arts. If you go to teach theatre in a school, college or university, you will be working in education first and admin second; the arts will be third.

Do your research. It's not the arts profession, it's the education system.

Of course they are linked, but know that one is not the other.

OPEN A SCHOOL?

I owned and ran an academy of my own for three years. I managed to hit the market just at the right time in the town I was living in. I also had a good reputation for producing decent community theatre, so when I did an open audition (open to any age), I had 180 people turn up. The spin on my business was that we'd stage three musicals a year and that students would learn through performance. It was fun and I learned a lot about what I was capable of – and my values. The academy had a beautiful spirit and many students went on to work in the arts and are still friends today.

It was not always enjoyable, obviously. Dealing with over one hundred personalities was a stretch, and producing three massive shows with costumes and sets with nearly eighty people in the cast definitely took its toll. It all ended on a happy note, though – as, when I left, the company was passed on to some members who carried it on for a few more years.

So, should you open your own school? First, do your research on your rivals, fees and available theatre spaces you can stage your work. Next, think about what you're offering that's unique to you – this is key. After that, you're going to need an infrastructure to support your ambitions. This could include chaperones, a company manager, wardrobe or publicity.

Go ahead if you feel the burn to do it, but know that it's exhausting and hugely time-consuming.

BUSKING

I've known a few buskers and they are remarkable beings.
They are the true vagabond tradesperson: trudging the streets
and setting up shop, singing for their supper.

Sound familiar?

SLOW PAYMENTS

Do not lie down if you are due a payment. If a venue or host is mucking you
around, call them on it. Calmly, of course – after all, you're a service provider
and deserve to be paid for your service. If they're playing a dirty game, talk to
your peers and find out if it's also happening to them.

Remember, always stay calm and professional. The moment you rant and start
using exclamation points you've lost some power.

Rise up, theatremakers – you are a business and venues *cannot* not pay you.

IT'S A SMALL WORLD

The UK theatre trade is small and if you stick around long enough it will become even smaller as you get to know everyone. Eventually, you'll all know the same people and will have haunted the same theatres and spaces at one time or another.

Make sure you behave.

INCOMPETENCE

I'm always amazed when I experience incompetence in the arts. As if our job and the quest to remain in it isn't hard enough; we still encounter a lack of basic skills and communication.

It's nothing unusual, as it's just incompetence, and unfortunately us artists are not immune.

TEACHING TEACHERS

I have taught or mentored teachers in many settings. It feels wonderful to share my skill set with teachers desperate for new strategies that they can use in the classroom.

If you ever get the chance, do try it. I think we come into our own when we show teachers how to teach a song or write a play, to choreograph a dance or produce a production. But, again, do your research. The idea of delivering the performing arts in a school is always wrapped up in great ideals, but the reality is that the way you administer an arts activity must never be overlooked. By this I mean, teaching how to execute an activity is different from just showing the activity.

EXTRAS WORK

Now, there is this myth that you cannot work as a main character on a TV show if you've been a 'supporting artist' on it. Of course, as always, this is an unproven theory uttered by an agent one day and then perpetuated by actors fearful that they will never work again. Some TV shows may have this policy, but more fool them if they reject the actor they really want, after learning that they once worked as an extra on their production. But I bet that has never happened.

I once got with an amazing company and when they learned I was reliable and could act, I started to get some really interesting jobs – so great even my 'full-time' actor friends were jealous of the stuff I appeared in.

You'll get to learn so much on set too – you really will. Yes, it can be taxing, but grit your teeth and focus on the money. Take some of your work with you and it'll be like someone's paying you to work whilst you're on a set.

A few other minor tips: take snacks, a book and a phone charger. Learn the third assistant director's name, and plan your journey meticulously so you're never late.

Other than that, just enjoy it.

OTHER WORK

Call any other work – the non-arts one – a particular
name. I just call it my other work, or other life. I think the
moment you start saying, 'I'm going to work', when you're
going to your 'other' job, you've fallen down a trap. Remind
yourself that the theatre is your work and everything else is a
sometimes necessary, temporary journey running alongside
for a limited period.

CRAP TV
SOMETIMES HEALS

Sit on the couch in your pants and eat some chips.

WHEN FRIENDS DISAGREE

I'll never forget walking out of what we were led to believe was 'The Best Musical in The World Ever'. The hype was massive and the CD was quite good too. Leaving Drury Lane, though, I felt quite low, like we'd all been cheated. I voiced this to my group of friends and one of them took quite an offence to my comment; so much so, they walked off.

Looking back, I stand by my statement as the show closed pretty quickly and, knowing what I know now some twenty years later, it was a show with a bunch of tricks – but no real content.

My friend's reaction is still interesting to me, though, as I think I hit a nerve that they couldn't or didn't want to voice because their reaction was, 'But they worked hard on this…' Of course they had, but that wasn't my criticism. In fact, for me, that made it worse – it meant they'd worked hard on the wrong area. Still, what do I know? Everyone's laughter and tears are valid.

TALENT

I'm not sure about this word any more. In fact it makes me want to vomit. It feels like it's been hijacked to recruit 'Stars of the Future' and the 'Next Big Thing'.

My suspicions were confirmed when the arbitrary concept 'gifted and talented' entered the UK schooling system. I remember looking in horror at my timetable, thinking, 'What's the criteria for this blessing? And gifted and talented… at what?'

Nowadays, I reframe talent as *ability*.

WHO'S YOUR NEMESIS?

I love playing this game. Grab a pen, a pad and some friends.

1. List anyone who's (metaphorically) stolen your career and why. Now write them a letter saying how much you admire them.

2. List which theatre company you wished you had invented. Now write them a letter telling them why you were so inspired by their last production.

3. Now swap them all around and read aloud each other's efforts.

IDOLS

You don't have to worship anyone.

230

THE SHORE

At some point in your career you'll start to find there is a pattern in your work: a theme maybe, or a style. Pay attention to these because sometimes the way we imagine our careers to be – or the way we want them to turn out – doesn't always chime with the way they actually are.

Look for the unconscious things you have created, search for their common ground – there is your shore. Keep it in sight, not to necessarily create work like that again, but to know it's always there if you want it.

231

JOURNALS AND DREAMS

Invest in a decent journal and a pen you like, and keep them separate from your show ones. This journal is just for the dialogue with yourself; for your dreams, for the digging down into your expectations, and your choices. Your day-to-day life may come into this one – it's all good, just let it flow. Keep it on the shelf and, when it's full, get another and another, and so on. They'll be fun to look back on and very useful when you need a creative shot in the arm.

TYPES OF STAGING

Thrust-staging is my favourite style of performance. I love the challenges and possibilities it conjures, and the audience experience can be super-interesting.

Again, I didn't realise this until later on in my career, as I was always imagining my work either in the round or traverse. What's your favourite and why? What does the trade need more of?

THEATRE IS HARD

Hug me.

YOUR HOME

Where you live is absolutely connected to your job. From the architecture to the location, from the people you live with to the town you're in: all of these are intrinsically linked to your well-being. Live in a house with conflicts, you'll find yourself jamming in your headphones trying to find some peace. Travel is dire? You'll just go out less or resent your home.

Now, I know that because of the financial juggling we must do to live a life in the arts, we can sometimes find that a temporary compromise may be useful, but it should be just that: temporary. Remember, you're allowed to expect things in life. Usher them in, make space for them – those high expectations. You'll be surprised how life starts to make good on your decisions.

SHOWCASES

Theatre courses are usually desperate for more audiences at their showcases, so contact the correct department and get your name on their list. This is where you get to see the next diamond in the rough.

YOUR PLACE AT THE TABLE

You will have to fight hard for your place at the table. It's not that you're not welcome; you are – the next big hit is always required. No, this thought is about the fact no one knows you exist until you do. And even when you have arrived, you'll still need to keep nudging your way in.

It's fine and, to be honest, I think everyone at all 'levels' has to do this at some point. Also, there is really no imaginary foe you must defeat – they are just in your head, these gods of theatre that occupy the space you think you should be in by now. Just resolve to remain relevant, important and necessary – the rest will come.

A DIFFERENT THEATRE

Of course, every year, the world changes. These past five years, the UK in particular seems to have run aground and been altered – permanently.

Anyway, it is what it is. Our job technically remains the same: to make theatre for the now. I'm excited to see what you will do for our trade.

BRISTOL, MANCHESTER, ETC.

London is the capital of the UK. That's a given and the city is a world leader in the arts. Yes, I believe the scales to be rebalancing, but London's heady concoction of history, culture, brand and size will always be out front in terms of where the focus goes. That's just common sense for a global-marketing strategy – to put your capital front and centre.

But of course, this is sometimes at the cost of so many other amazing theatre ventures that are just as innovative, if not more so, but don't get enough traction inside our cultural zeitgeist. Cambridge Junction, The Wardrobe Theatre, Slung Low or Old Joint Stock – how many of us know they exist? How about The Town and Gown in Cambridge, Eden Court in Inverness, Macrobert Arts Centre in Stirling, The Ardhowen Theatre in Enniskillen, The Torch Theatre Company in Pernbrokeshire and The Frinton Summer Theatre? School yourself – it can only nourish our trade as you broaden your horizons.

GIFT OF THE GAB

Now, before we close this section I want to quickly shine a light on the theory that you must have the gift of the gab to wing it, to con, to cajole – and to find a way to get where you're going by owning everyone, every room, and everything. Is this true, though?

I'm quite a quiet, reserved soul and tend to hate the hard sell or the schmoozing of things. I'm better in small groups and can have anxiety issues in big crowds talking about something I've made. I've gotten better over the years, but when I compare myself to some of my friends who can walk into a room and own it, I'm a shrinking violet.

I think both approaches work on different levels. Yes, the confident approach in a social situation can be the right choice – but ultimately the work, the theatre, your artistic work (if it speaks to the now), will hold the room for you long after the curtain has come down. So don't worry if you're not a social butterfly – many of us aren't.

YOUR THOUGHTS

So, how do you feel?

I have to say that I've learned loads writing this section. Not only about the trade but how I feel about it. Plus, I've also realised I actually do have a method – a sort of practice – that I now use to make theatre.

PART 5

MAKING
A CAREER

This final chapter talks to the entrepreneur inside of you and offers up ways to keep your artistic spirit nourished. It's a tricky thing, sustaining a career in the arts. Even now, at the age of fifty, I still question if I have made the right decision. The message of society is to seek out security and safety in life and that anything else is just simply weird, and then that system demands that by a certain age you must be content with everything you've achieved, sit in a chair and watch the world go by. Fine, if that's for you; godspeed. Not me, though. I want to watch the world go by now, whilst I'm still young enough to learn from it, and then make live art that discusses it. And I don't want it to ever stop.

I know that, having tried the other options, I am only happy living this life I lead today, and it was the one I wanted as a teenager. A life filled with creativity, fun, interesting people, stories, magic; but above all: freedom. As a freelance artist I consider myself to be free because I do not seek the things the majority are – seemingly – aiming for. It's because I don't know where I'll be next year or the year after, that I love my life so much, because

no matter what comes along, I can turn around and say I identified my calling and stuck with it. It doesn't matter to me that I don't own anything fancy because I have a rich life with good friends. It doesn't matter to me that I haven't worked at the National Theatre because it's not my goal (if it happens, it happens); and it doesn't matter to me that I'm an outsider looking into the world and seeing all its problems as that's where I want to be, because then, and only then, can I assemble stories that will discuss the issues I've identified.

To run against this narrative (and believe me, that's exactly what you will be doing) is very challenging, but if it's truly the direction that you are heading in (having announced that you wish to work in the arts), then you must accept early on – and I mean truly accept it – that you're going to need to foster some fairly unshakeable tunnel vision, an immense skill to duck and dive social expectations, and that you'll always be seen as the child that never grew up. Which is why this last chapter is me offering up some thoughts on how to sustain a career in the arts.

MONEY

It's a trick to balance the type of work you want to make with the jobs you may need for the cash. I remember attending a talk by Rufus Norris, Artistic Director of the National Theatre, and he said not to do a job just for the money because you'll end up resenting it. I remember thinking at the time, 'Yeah, easy to say – less easy to do.' However, I do know what he means – or at least the intention of it.

When I reflect upon the jobs that I've done only for the money I have found myself in situations where I'm either unhappy or frustrated, or just doing repetitive stuff that I've done over and over. Being in a role that I'm way overqualified for is also a sign that my objectives may have been skewed.

The only person who can answer this for you is you, but I think it's useful to identify what you will and won't do for the money.

HOW TO CRITIQUE THEATRE

It's easy for me to sit in an audience and criticise another artist's work. As I mature, though, and make more original theatre, I am super-conscious that unless I start to interrogate my thoughts a little bit more every time I see another person's show, I may artistically run aground myself. If I learn to run towards empathy first, every time, I will remind myself that making theatre is hard.

So now I ask, 'What was their original intention?' 'What did they intend to make?' 'Did it work?' And, ultimately (as an audience member), 'Was I served?'

AGENTS

I've never had a long-term agent. I tried once, but never really thought of them as a career option because I wasn't that keen on running around London vying for a job in (mostly) commercials. Why? I like my freedom and, once I got into that system, I felt like a product and not a person. Yes, the money would be nice, but so would winning the lottery – and honestly, what are the chances?

If one day I build a larger profile or possess a body of work that needs managing, then it might be useful to have someone to deal with contracts and act as a firewall for me, but currently I'm not sure what one can offer me that I can't create by myself.

You watch, I'll get one after this has been published.

THE SELF-APPOINTED

…are everywhere.

PROJECT

…your voice. Why? Because you'll be in a class of your own; and a lost art will be rediscovered. I don't care if you have a microphone, speak up.

YOU'VE ARRIVED

You're here. You made it. Your show is a huge global success.

Now what?

Please return to Thought #1.

LABELS

Some of my friends call me 'the worst gay man ever'
– a phrase that always concerns me. I get what they're
implying, though: that I don't fit with the expected type (the
stereotype) for a gay man.

Years ago you either had to be camp or just stay inside the
closet – there was no middle ground in some people's minds.
I guess 'we' were deemed safe if we were camp or funny.
But my young brain clocked early on that this rule was used
by scared heterosexuals wishing to make us more palatable.
I, however, was good at rugby and wasn't one for Kylie's
catalogue – further confounding the stereotype. (She does
seem nice, though.)

Anyway, godspeed to everyone, and I'm not sure this is
the place to unpack the politics of this, but one thing I do
recognise is that I don't like labels that are given to me by
society nor the trade. I'm me. Russell Lucas.

STRATEGY

How do you want to make theatre?

My favourite way of working is in small groups with a common purpose and, for the most part, trying to subvert some expectations along the way. This could be by way of rethinking a venue's traditional space, digging down into what a genre is about, or challenging the audience's expectations.

What's your ideal environment like?

LAZY INCLUSION

I'm very conscious when applying for a job where filling in a section that reveals who I sleep with will somehow contribute to my getting the job. How scary is that? I want a job for my skill set and ideas and not have them sidelined by aggressive equal-opportunity rosters. I demand to live in a world where institutions apply their intellect and social consciousness rather than be guided by lazy forms so they don't actually have to engage.

THERAPY

I interviewed a director friend of mine a while back for
my YouTube channel, and in the interview she shared her
thoughts on some of the politically and socially sensitive
situations she had found herself in over the years. (She'd
made community work in Rwanda and Lebanon, to name
but a few.) She then concluded by saying that she'd realised
'I'm a theatremaker, not a therapist.' I would have screamed
with joy, but we were filming.

How did this all come about? When did artist-led therapy
become a thing and when was it accepted that we can
execute our job under this banner without qualifications
or experience? Why do we automatically think we are
therapists?

I have definitely found myself on occasion in situations
where a qualified arts therapist should have been leading
the room instead of me. Of course, I can manage empathy
and sensitivity, but when did we get so lost up the outreach
road? I suspect it's a result of the artist being wheeled out as
'the creative one'; but by putting us into potentially tricky or
volatile situations it seems unsafe to assume that some magic
will occur just because I bang a gong.

I worked for one 'arts' company where I ended up teaching
sessions to teenagers about Class A drugs. Oh boy, was that
a mistake. Not only was I ill-equipped, but I was extremely
let down by the company that employed me. They posted
a few lame resources and some basic info to me and
suddenly I was raised up to be the creative drugs expert in a
secondary school.

It paid so well it took every ounce of my soul to remove
myself from it, as I'd become dependent on the cash flow,
but thankfully my lighthouse brought me back to my shore.

WORK EVERY DAY

Here's that word again: 'Work'. What is work? You can work on your abs to make them more defined, work on your car and your college degree. Then there's the other work – the one that you do for fast money.

What I want you to pledge to yourself today is that these two uses of the word become the same. That from now on you will work on your art to make a career that you will make money on. That you will work on your business skills, writing, directing, etc. every day, and all just for you and your one primary goal: to work in the arts as a professional artist. Block off days or times in your diary for your work – and don't feel guilty about not going out with your mates all the time. Tell them you're working. Feels weird, doesn't it?

Theatre is not your hobby.

YOU'RE ALLOWED

There will always be a tiny part of you that will not completely believe that you can work in theatre. That you're seemingly surrounded by people who are allowed – and know that they're allowed. In fact, they appear to never question it; they were just born to be where they are. You may suspect that they see you as the runt of the litter and that everyone expects you to go back home at some point and open your own ballet school or work in a youth summer camp.

But I'm not interested in what they think of you. What I want you to ask yourself is: 'Am I internalising other people's expectations?' or 'Am I subliminally planning to give up because that's much easier?' (It's not, by the way.)

Whatever your path, don't blame any imaginary system for how you're progressing, because you're the one that holds the compass. Yes, it might need recalibrating on occasion, but crack on.

SOME BOOKS FOR YOU

Some of these chime with my thoughts on finding a way to do the thing you want to do by yourself. Others are ones that have inspired me.

On Directing: Interviews with Directors edited by Gabriella Giannachi and Mary Luckhurst

Notes from the Field by Anna Deavere Smith

A Better Direction: A national enquiry into the training of directors for theatre, film and television by Kenneth Rea

This Time Together: Laughter and Reflection by Carol Burnett

The Empty Space by Peter Brook

Directing the Action by Charles Marowitz

The Art of Acting by Stella Adler

True and False: Heresy and Common Sense for the Actor by David Mamet

Deep Are the Roots: Trailblazers Who Changed Black British Theatre by Stephen Bourne

Becoming Richard Pryor by Scott Saul

Devising Theatre: A Practical and Theoretical Handbook by Alison Oddey

British Asian Theatre: Dramaturgy, Process and Performance by Dominic Hingorani

The Necessary Theatre by Peter Hall

Mainstream AIDS Theatre, the Media, and Gay Civil Rights: Making the Radical Palatable by Jacob Juntunen

Mis-directing the Play: An Argument Against Contemporary Theatre by Terry McCabe

Born Standing Up: A Comic's Life by Steve Martin

The UK Scriptwriter's Survival Handbook or (How to Earn an Actual Living as a Writer) by Tim Clague and Danny Stack

Intercultural Aesthetics in Traditional Chinese Theatre: From 1978 to the Present by Wei Feng

YOUR OPENING

You know that moment when you are in the audience about to watch a show? It's about ten minutes before the curtain goes up and you're idle. Take a look around. Look at the rigging, the design and the ushers. Now feel the atmosphere and ask yourself, 'What is everyone expecting at 7:30 p.m?'

Now, you – as a professional theatremaker – will more than likely have a different agenda to the regular theatregoer, but put it aside for a moment and ask yourself, 'What's the regular person next to me looking forward to?'

After this, imagine your work opening on this stage. How will you open it in response to what you are feeling right now? How will you serve them?

NO FUNDS?
FIND A WAY

Without any financial support or personal funds, what else have you got? What is at your disposal?

Some free space somewhere? A large room in your house? A church hall? A Scout hut? Friends with any of these? Social media to ask for some free space? Crowdfunding options? Wealthy friends? Storytelling skills you can barter with a primary school to use one of their rooms?

What can you offer? Open rehearsals? Put a small advert in your local paper for free space? Tweet to local prolific actors? Get yourself interviewed in your local paper about the lack of arts in your area? Start a Facebook page? Follow a page that offers free stuff?

Never throw your hands up in the air. Keep picking at the rather dull, restrictive narrative of 'I can't afford it.'

AND...

Never throw your hands up in the air.

Ask 'What can I do?'

11 SENTENCES YOU'LL ALWAYS HEAR

1. 'When are you going to settle down?'
2. 'So you're fringe?'
3. 'You're *still* in the theatre?'
4. 'You should be in that soap opera.'
5. 'Have I seen you in anything?'
6. 'You still do that actor-y thing?'
7. 'Yeah, but there's no money in it, is there?'
8. 'But what do you *do*?'
9. 'But it's not West End, is it?'
10. 'And what do you do for money?'
11. 'What's your real job?'

SITTING ON THE COUCH

If you ever find that you are worried about income for the next six months, remind yourself that you're not going to be sitting on the couch for that time. Your resourcefulness will kick in because you have decided you're in it for the long haul, and bumps in the road towards our goals are always going to happen, no matter what profession we're in.

Face them, deal with them, and don't let them break you. Yes, you may run aground on occasion, but rest assured that you will look back at these moments and realise it was worth weathering the storm.

YOUTH THEATRE

Having spent many years in this sector I can say, with authority, youth theatre can be a life-saver for a lot of young people.

Like all education, though, if you want to work in it, remember it will also have one foot firmly in social care. You will be their teacher, of course, but some young people need youth-theatre initiatives for other reasons that are not theatrical ones. You may be surrounded by fifty students but only a few have natural ability or will actually want to work in the arts. You will still have a role in this setting; just check you are passionate about all of the duties the job entails.

FAME

Whenever you read a programme in the theatre it is a given that each artist involved in the production will always announce their big hitters in their biog. The prolific venues, the famous names, and the noted productions will all be brought out.

Now, if you have curated a career based on what interests you, you may not have created a bankable, sellable or even very jazzy biography like another actor in the programme, but don't worry about it. You have nothing to prove. Remain confident that you still have credibility. You are a professional theatremaker and your performance can be just as arresting as someone who once understudied Judi Dench's spear carrier.

NAKED THEATRE

Ah, the classic dream. The curtain goes up and you have no clothes on… or you don't know your lines… or both. I still get these dreams and have learned that they are really about my responsibility, my power and the anxiety created around performing.

If you are the performer in a show, you are the manager of everything and everyone. You must balance the plot, please the writer, appease the director, work with the other actors, entertain the audience, smile at the producer every minute of the day, remember your lines, remember your props, watch the lights, serve the space, speak the truth, wear different clothes, prepare – and make it all look flawless.

Anxiety is your discipline keeping you on, and in, your game.

WORKSHOP JUNKIES

I knew a performer a few years ago and they were always at some sort of workshop. Clowning, casting, movement, voice; you name it, they'd be on it. Whilst on one level I applauded their willingness to try everything out, they never actually worked as a performer. They completed their degree and then got hooked into what I call 'workshop addiction'.

Now, of course, every artist must try and do a few workshops from time to time to keep their creative muscles ripped, but I did worry that by being surrounded by other actors in a workshop, my friend had convinced themselves they were working in the theatre, when they did everything but.

In the end, they became a life coach.

DRAMA SCHOOLS

Seems strange to use just the word drama, doesn't it? Students study every mode of performance, yet they still call themselves a 'drama' school?

I wonder if they should reconfigure and call themselves 'theatre schools'? It's the same in secondary schools with their 'drama department'. Students do not go into the drama trade; they go into the theatre trade.

Tell you what – I decree that we shall all start to call them 'theatre schools' and 'theatre departments' from now on. There, I've renamed them all.

Theatre has arrived in our schools. Exciting.

COMMERCIALS

There's a Faustian pact between the performer and the advertising sector; it's just a question of if you can see it or not.

Appearing in a television commercial is about actors wanting to earn a lot of dough very quickly. But it's not the real you acting, it's your 'other' self. Keep them separate.

Okay, you may find yourself in Dubai soaking up the rays, counting your tens of thousands of pounds, thinking that you've made it – but it's not your real acting. Rest assured, though, Mephistopheles will come to collect your soul at some point. Just don't give him your real one.

TV

TV is such a great medium for actors. If you're lucky to be on a show (especially if it's a long-running show), they are well-oiled machines that run like clockwork. They tend to refresh crews often enough to keep everyone on their toes, and the permanent cast is usually so happy to see a new actor, they'll dote on you.

When I did extras work I learned early on that TV was better for me. It was quick, easy and you knew it was mostly over by 6 p.m. Whether you're a walk-on, a guest actor or heavily featured, you'll be treated well and work a short day for the most part. Grab the chance with both hands.

Extras jobs on commercials are the worst part of a supporting artist's life so I personally avoided them.

FILM

As a supporting artist (extra), I wasn't a fan of films. They are huge beasts with so much at stake daily that I felt like such a non-thing. Some extras would actually sign in and not do the job. They'd find a place to sleep or work and avoid the third assistant director.

Don't get me wrong, I enjoyed the work; I had some memorable moments on set – for *Skyfall* amongst others – and there's some very funny footage of me making silly faces behind Steve Coogan that made it into the final cut in a film I'll never reveal,* but they were less fun for me.

Now, if you get a larger role in movies then go read up about them as I've never done them. From the outside it seems like the actor's journey for films will be the same as for TV, only there'll be more of a detailed casting process – the film industry's pressure is next level.

* *The Look of Love.*

FALSE GODS

In this post-Covid world, it's becoming more and more evident that we really cannot rely on anything in our forever-threadbare trade. Arts spaces have closed, agents have fallen, casting directors who aren't in the inner-circles have folded, and middle-managers may be unemployed for a decade.

Add to this the creeping feeling that some unions, organisations and institutions have also lost actors' respect, casting sites have drip-fed and monetised performers out of their own game, and (now more than ever) the mainstream has closed its gates and run back towards that which they know – selling tickets fast – in order to survive.

So, now that you are calling the shots once again, what do you want? Some of the false gods you have worshipped have had their curtains pulled back, revealing to you a space. Now what?

THE BOSS

If, for whatever reason, something goes wrong, there's nowhere else to lay the blame except at your own feet. You are the boss – it's with you that the buck stops.

Of course, some things are out of your control, but if you find yourself howling in the air with frustration, take a moment and reflect on what you would do differently next time.

Remember, no system is targeting you. If you use the term 'they' then you may have to reassess and reset your mind a little. There is no 'they'. It's *you* that must create the stories and do the work towards this.

It's just 'you'.

16 FREELANCING THOUGHTS

1. Work Monday to Sunday with some time off.
2. Always reply to every email. Always.
3. Avoid laying in bed for too long.
4. Exercise and eat well.
5. Weigh up alcohol's after-effects.
6. Learn everyone's job.
7. Create most days (you're allowed).
8. Give yourself a random day off just because you can.
9. Keep a record of your work-relevant purchases.
10. Have an up-to-date CV ready to go at all times and make sure your online presence is current.
11. Communicate your expectations to yourself and others.
12. Foster the habit of listing activities to be completed.
13. Live in a space that makes you happy.
14. Work in cash-cow jobs that are linked to your main work.
15. Have a professional signature at the end of your email with your job title under your name.
16. Balance work and relationships wisely.

THE IVY LEE
METHOD

There is a very famous work strategy called the Ivy Lee Method and it goes like this...

List the six things you need to do tomorrow in order of importance:

1. Finish book.
2. Exercise.
3. Follow up on email to a client.
4. Complete invoice.
5. Plan September's rehearsals.
6. Learn lines.

If by the end of your day you haven't completed all of the list you nudge the outstanding ones over to the next day and add more to retain the six-point structure. I find this method eases any worries I have for the next day and allows me to switch off at night.

TRAINING BEGINS

When students graduate, some (on occasion) think that it is the end of their training; that they've peaked. I'm telling you now – in fact, no, I'm warning you – if you don't keep your performing muscle up to scratch, your neglect will be noticeable and could directly affect the opportunities offered to you.

The performers that cut through the rest are the devoted, professional, humble and highly skilled wordsmiths. Be that person.

No excuses. Find a way to remain actively creative every day. You're allowed.

DO EVERYTHING

Try everything in the arts trade. If you can get into a clowning class or a short lighting workshop, do it. If there's a Commedia dell'Arte or mime session, go for it. Look for directing, producing, sound and writing initiatives too. All of these will equip you for your future as a theatremaker – and that can only be a plus, right?

Challenge yourself too. If you don't know how something works and probably should, sort it out. You're the boss.

ENTITLEMENT

If you begin by presuming that your show will sell, you could be dead in the water from the beginning. I've seen it happen. Performers convinced they will sell out their show once they've handed out a few flyers but, sadly, it's not true.

The reality is that sometimes shows just don't sell. No matter your financial backing, your work may not hit the world at the right moment and your life-changing idea may not tap into the vein.

Don't presume anything. All bets are off and it's a very competitive market.

MONTHLY MINDS

The regular working world is built on monthly signifiers, and the paycheque at the end of it is the biggest one of all. In theory, this supports your monthly bills and outgoings, but if you're a freelancer that mindset needs to be jettisoned pretty sharpish. It just doesn't work like that, and you'll get some deep anxiety every thirty days if you don't tap into the financial rhythms of freelance life.

As a working professional artist, you will create work and also take work in response to your life requirements. Because of this randomness, these jobs will pay as and when.

I've found for the most part that everyone is decent and pays me within the month, but obviously there are a few bodies that don't – who then get a black mark against their name and a strongly worded (professional) email from me saying: 'Pay up now.'

The transition from monthly-brain to whenever-mind is a trick. I think I mastered it a few years ago when I had accumulated enough work that dropped little money bags into my account at random moments. Think of them as drip-feed payments. Yes, it's not as tidy, but it's the same concept: you work, you get paid.

YOUTUBE

275

I recently started a YouTube channel. It was something I'd wanted to do for a while because I like talking to people about their theatremaking careers. I also like to talk to people we haven't heard from before; the grassroots theatremakers (the majority), where you are more than likely to live and work.

I understand why we see the same faces interviewed over and over under the title 'expert', but they're not the ones who are trudging the streets with one suitcase on a show they made with fifty pence that's selling out venues. (Yes, that's a thing and a possibility.)

It was after refining this book idea that I thought I'd also like to interview 300 theatremakers, so I've begun. And I will do it. It's my new job.

Why now? Because there's very little, free theatre-based content online from the UK that is not hosted by a prolific theatre or focused on the sale of a ticket. So, *300 Thoughts from Theatremakers* is going to be a library of 300 interviews for anyone who wants them in the future. Check me out.

MY INVESTMENTS

I've spoken about this before (Thought #111: Invest) but I thought I'd share some of my investments I've made over the last few years:

A new computer: My old one was free but very tired, so I knew – given all I had planned in my head – I needed to invest in a new, powerful computer to enable my visions. I'd just done a lucrative creative teaching job abroad so I reinvested some of those earnings back into my next project.

Final Cut and Final Draft software: I needed Final Cut on my computer to deal with the edits of my YouTube channel and to enable me to take my work to the next level. Final Draft is an industry-standard screenwriting programme and I had an offer code for £30 off. I jumped on it and taught myself how to write screenplays. It's early days, but I love it.

Speakers and a microphone: I work with music a lot in my practice so I needed to have a portable system for rehearsals. It's basically a karaoke set, but it was only fifty quid for the mic, stand and speakers.

Phone: I updated my phone so I could film footage for shows. I did my research and found that a lot of professional filmmakers are now using particular phones to make movies. Yes, *movies*. I had made some money from a web series I made and so bought my phone with that.

FLUX

You may, on occasion, feel frozen. Unpack it. There may be no artistic project on the horizon, your income may have slowed down, and there's nothing of major social importance in the diary.

I am getting better at living inside this, so when it arrives I try to live in my flux, my inertia, and its static state. Try to rest inside these alternative universes – journal at your side at all times, of course.

RESOURCES AND INNOVATORS

American Theatre Wing's YouTube channel (for the interviews).

HowlRound.com (for the independent articles and online content).

DV8 Physical Theatre performances on YouTube (to see narrative in movement).

Stella Adler teaching on YouTube (to watch her demand responsibility from the actor).

David Mamet directing on YouTube (to watch him actioning his theories).

Any performance by Sylvie Guillem (a ballet icon).

New Earth Theatre for their platforming of stories by British East and South East Asians.

Company Three for their refreshing approach to making theatre with young people.

Galactik Ensemble on YouTube (physical marvels).

Olivier de Sagazan on YouTube (performance art in its truest form).

Anything about or by The Wardrobe Ensemble (study their journey).

Scene & Heard for their groundbreaking work with young playwrights.

Kali Theatre for their work by South Asian women.

Anything you can find on Anna Deavere Smith for her techniques in making theatre.

Anything by Joyce Grenfell you can find for her songs, joy, cheekiness, and her writing.

Seek out the film *Black Theater: The Making of a Movement*.

Unsplash for free images/footage.

The V&A for their recorded theatre archive.

…and, of course, 300 Thoughts from Theatremakers on YouTube.

EVOLVE

The nuances within us all are evident when in the creative space. Some of us will be deft at dialogue, others swift with on-the-spot ideas.

I have always deemed myself to be a good organiser of things, and that has translated into having a flare for direction. It's not something I was taught – I just have an instinct for making ideas happen coherently and then forming them into a production. It's the same when I perform; I know how to move my body and use my voice in particular ways to usher in a performance with a required outcome. As time has trundled on, though, I have become more and more interested in writing.

Having reached a natural junction by which point I had observed a lot of writers, I thought, 'Okay – I think I can do that too.' Writing also requires form, direction, and the movement of things to create a whole. I also adore writing dialogue.

So where are you off to next? Does your dance push you into mime? Will your producing skills usher you into publishing plays? How about using your love of people and make a short film using soundbites of their lives?

Jump over all the walls and cross the streams. We need you.

ENABLERS

It's a trick to spot the people who are good for you.

When I think back on who has inspired me – and I'm not talking about the famous here – I have images of relatives long gone or vague, nostalgic ideas of places, films, music and art.

I have a second cousin who is much older than me and when I was ten he was probably about twenty. Our family would be visiting his house and he would waft in with his long beard and transient spirit. He was heavily into vinyl and was also an artist. Obviously, I no longer wanted to hang out with my boring family and just wanted to go and live with him on his boat. He had a deep effect on me and I see now why that was: he wasn't the norm, and I didn't – and still don't – wish to be either.

I've spoken before about how music is always in my life; it nurtures and supports me in every minute of the day. Film, however, holds a very particular space too. I grew up in the video era, so experienced the time where you could record and watch films at will on your TV. It was a magical time and filmmakers finally had a direct line to their audiences. In primary school, we would secretly swap our parents' horror films around the classroom until one of us was found out – or until the pipeline dried up.

Those few years were so fertile for me. To see all that creativity and possibility in front of me helped my writing. I will never forget in secondary school I wrote a sequel to *A Nightmare on Elm Street* and my amazing English teacher gave me an A. What a visionary she was, because although I had used a pop-culture film as my genesis – she'd spotted my passion. Film and Mrs Durand enabled me.

Delve deep and name your enablers.

EXCITEMENT!

This is slightly linked to my thoughts on showbiz (Thought #181).

When writing your copy for a show, sending an email or writing a social-media post, check in with any desire to use an exclamation point. I think the world may have reached peak mediocrity and no longer sees, nor needs, any more of them.

The exc!amat!on po!nt these days !s mean!ngless! !t doesn't muster that wh!ch !t was designed for. !t merely shows a lack of !magination and ! feel patron!sed now whenever ! see it.

Here's a lovely rule: the first rule of exclamation points is, don't use them.

ARTEFACTS

I have anxiety about all of the theatre sets that are either abandoned or in storage. What did they all mean and what are they now?

Surely the set matters only at the moment when it's being used. That the grand falling chandelier is only relevant as it is raised to the ceiling and when it falls again. When those two things are done, it's just a dead, albeit clever, prop.

What I believe remains after the theatrical experience is what the work induced in the audience, because it's an experience that we provide which is intangible and indescribable, but (hopefully) forever emblazoned on their memory.

How do we conjure this every time? Well, you'll find your way.

BARRIERS

One of my biggest barriers to working in the arts was my mother.

She, like most parents, wanted only the best things for me, and so when she realised I was serious about studying and then actually working in the arts, my mum, in a lot of ways, became my biggest enemy. Now, of course, I loved her dearly and if she were still around she'd be mortified that I felt like this, but in some ways she made me bloody well continue, because I knew what I was talking about and I knew that she didn't. She was not equipped with the knowledge that I had: that you can work in the arts forever, you just have to want a different life.

Of course, as the child always seeks parental approval, I definitely ran aground a few times on my quest, but something kept driving and pushing me back to the theatre, and eventually – once she saw me on stage and then becoming a theatre lecturer with a regular salary – she was totally on board.

I soon lost her selective-approval, though, when I gave it all up and became freelance. Even in my thirties I would still have her on the phone saying, 'What about your washing?' 'London's full of weirdos, come home.' What she failed to realise was, I was home.

SELF-SABOTAGE

We all have our little sins or indulgent behaviours that we probably shouldn't do. Mine is drinking wine.

Silly, aren't they, the things that we know aren't really good for us, but we do anyway. However, I think in our trade in particular, we have to keep an eye on these sins of ours, because our body and its output are our job's biggest asset. Why would we go and sabotage our rehearsal period – or worse still – our show, for the sake of a short-term kick?

So, how can we manage? Well, that's up to you, but do you know what I've learned? Something has to go if you're not running on a full tank, or else your work, your profession and your career could be in jeopardy.

YOUR PATH

Alongside your weekly or daily plan, you could also try doing a yearly or even a life plan.

Try this exercise…

'What do I want this year?'

List everything you wish to achieve in the next twelve months.

Now extend that to five years, ten, and then twenty. Write a paragraph or two, or a list – whatever works for you. Allow anything you like on the list. It could be anything from a sell-out show to having children. Be honest with yourself and don't feel any shame in your desires – it's only you who will ever see this list.

Once you've completed it, circle the goals based in the arts and then see what you have. Any surprises in there?
I did it last year and it was funny as two of the things were both achieved by Christmas.*

* I wanted a long beard and to write a screenplay.

286

FINANCIAL WIZARDRY

As an artist you will be a super-flexible financial wizard, a sage of all things cheap that will include free or very reasonably priced tickets. But where can we get them?

Nowadays there are about four or five websites and apps that give out free or cheap seats on the day. Some theatres, including prolific ones, do a one-pound seat. Yes, you read that correctly. They don't advertise them, but you can rock up to a space just before the curtain goes up and get a seat for a pound. Do a deep web search and you'll find the methods others have employed to obtain these gems.

Oh, and make coffee at home rather than spend three quid on one.

287

CONTRIBUTE

Giving back to the trade will be one of the most important things you will ever do. It's as important as the making of theatre.

PARENTS

Parents, quite rightly, want to protect their children. They want us to succeed, to have a job, to have a roof over our heads, and to be financially solvent. It seems, though, that the arts needs better PR because none of the above is synonymous with our trade. No matter how many times I reminded my family of the ways to make money and the techniques I employed to remain solvent, they really couldn't connect it back to arts work. (Dreams were for the rich, remember?)

I think this issue will not be resolved swiftly; it seems to be deeply rooted in the British embarrassment and underestimation of the power of its live-arts heritage. A curious disease indeed: waiting for its world-beating theatre to grow up and get a real job.

So how can we ignore this relentless critique? Well, I think first, we should be mindful we don't internalise it, and second, we can do our parents double-proud by living lives of happiness while becoming game-changing theatremakers.

WALK AWAY

There's a lot of power in saying no.

If a job doesn't feel right then it's okay to walk away. Sometimes, by abandoning a project, we may give ourselves back some freedom by announcing out loud: 'This isn't working for me.' Yes, you do lose the job, but that will be filled with a new one soon enough – you are a resourceful professional who will not be sitting on the couch.

AVOID CHANGE

You cannot seek to change an audience. You can only present something and then let them deal with it how they want to. Thinking you can change an audience is arrogant; it carries intellectual weight only in your own head, not in anyone else's.

You may, however, be able to present some new thinking.

NEVER EMERGE

In the past ten years, someone somewhere coined the term 'emerging artist'. Never emerge, my friends, because this market-speak will have you mid-career at twenty and on the intellectual scrap-heap by twenty-one.

Of course, if you feel the urge to apply for something that is targeted at enabling your work then go for it, but never let anyone call you 'the next best thing', 'the emerging artist' or 'the hot young actor'. You're a professional theatremaker and always will be.

PREPARE

t doesn't matter if you don't :ome from money – or if you have 1one – you are still a professional heatremaker, because even when :ou are not earning cash, you are :onstantly working on honing your :raft. You do all this because one day you will be in a room, surrounded by the wealthy, the affluent or the prolific who presume they've been experts since birth – and you will need to hold your own.

You'll do fine.

CASH COWS

A few cash cow jobs that may interest you:

Modelling
Creative writing
Writing creative lesson plans for teachers
Teaching theatre
Teaching teachers creatively
Copywriting
Delivering in youth-theatre settings
Creating online media content
Working with a theatre's education department
Acting on film
Commercials
Voice-over
Coaching
Workshops
Writing articles/copy
Children's entertainment
Assistant jobs (director, producer, etc.)
Arts admin

ARTIST? ME?

Being the type of artist you wish to see in the trade is going to be the most gratifying experience ever.

I am the type of person that wishes to engage with – and then seriously prod – received wisdom both within theatre and the zeitgeist. I am of the mind that theatremakers who make art with very few resources have the most interesting stories and are probably following the defter of two paths (indie versus commercial). My Twitter account is fashioned to do exactly that and my existence (profile) is fairly low-key, but maybe enough to get me in a room.

That's exactly what I want. It's not about me, but my ideas. Interrogate your quest.

1,000 SHOWS

We all have a thousand ideas. Just walking down the street I can come up with a pitch for a small movie or a play. Of course, these fleeting ideas may never come off, but it proves my brain is fertile and telling itself stories. Only the other night I remembered my dad found a relative in the bath with a bottle of gin and by her side he found a dead parrot. That's a short film if ever I saw one.

Get your journal out and write your ideas down. *All of them.*

COMPROMISE

When you know something is right but you have to give in because other things are at stake, it is a tough pill to swallow. I get this when I'm a director and working with a writer and I know (as the outside eye) some of the decisions they have made aren't quite chiming with the overall landscape and won't translate into the live act so well.

When I come across these situations I never stay quiet, but I do try and find a practical way to explain my thoughts because then at least the writer will have the option to listen to or ignore me. If the issue is still there when we're back in the rehearsal room, sometimes the acting of the text in rehearsals will bring it back to the surface, which is obviously very useful for further discussions. If the thing I wanted to change survives into the production, I may learn that it was something over nothing and that I'd just got bogged down with it.

Whatever the outcome, remember you're not out to 'win', so you may need to bite your tongue on occasion – but make sure you've spoken up and made your peace with it.

TALKING

When asked how she became so rich and famous, Oprah Winfrey replied: 'Talking.'

I found this to be such a beautiful response; she did not set out to make millions of dollars, it just happened because she likes listening and learning from others.

Her follow-up answer? 'People like to talk and I like to listen.' That has stuck with me; there's something in it – I think it's humanity – that tells us that if we reach out and ask people about their lives, they will tell us; and therein lie the greatest stories.

SELL YOURSELF

Your resourcefulness may take you into teaching online or sharing a show you've made through YouTube. This is a smart move to keep the money coming in, but be wary of how much you monetise; the moment you start to sell yourself you may become someone that only makes their money by giving all their creative juices away, and it's important that you keep some things for yourself.

THE MARATHON

It's never going to stop, this journey you have chosen. This is it. There is no end, merely some pit-stops along the way (mostly you having a holiday or dealing with a life-event).

You'll always be on the horse, blindfolded and without a map. But if you can tune in to all your other senses, then you're in the race. By feeling your way through, you will find this trade giving you back a heightened perception and new-found insight; and like a finely tuned radar, you'll know what the world needs now, and what it will need next.

A GLOBAL
THEATREMAKER

Now we have reached the last thought, I hope that some of my thinking has seeped through into your 'practice', 'process', 'method' or 'ideas' – whatever you want to call it.

I didn't think I had a method until I wrote this book, but it seems it is to make theatre for the *now*; that if I hold myself and my ideas to ransom enough, exciting theatre will evolve into something relevant; it will also tighten and focus my future choices.

This, for me, is what the modern theatremaker must do – especially now in our conflicted, seemingly backward-looking world, desperate for change but resisting any forward motion.

The artist must live within the nuance of the world's discussions and, if we are to bring people together into a theatre (the seeing, the listening and the live space) and serve them as the audience, we must also dissect our logic, label our intentions and manage our egos.

The theatre *is* yours, but it's also theirs.

Thanks

My journey has been assisted and inspired by the following people…

To Pam Lumsden, Steph Coleman and Alan Harris for always insisting us students perform as much as possible and for being so intrinsic to the way I think about theatre and where I am today. Thank you so much.

To Sarah Wright-Owens and Mark Meylan for helping me to develop my singing voice.

To Katya Kamotskaia and Albert Filozov for unleashing my inner voice.

To all my Shropshire allies with whom I have worked or who have supported me over the years. You're the best and I'm eternally grateful.

To Sarah-Louise Young for upping my game every time we are in the room together.

To Sarita for sitting down and just chewing the fat whenever I need it.

To Orna and Alanna for being in the room with me and questioning everything.

And finally, to my mum and dad. I'm here, which means you are too.